USE

The activities in this book are designed for independent use by students who have had instruction in the specific skills covered in the lessons. Copies of the activity sheets can be given to individuals or pairs of students for completion. When students are familiar with the content of the worksheets, they can be assigned as homework.

To begin, determine the implementation that fits your students' needs and your classroom structure. The following plan suggests a format for this implementation.

1. **Administer** the Assessment Test to establish baseline information on each student. This test may also be used as a post-test when a student has completed a unit.

2. **Explain** the purpose of the worksheets to the class.

3. **Review** the mechanics of how you want students to work with the activities. Do you want them to work in pairs? Are the activities for homework?

4. **Introduce** students to the process and purpose of the activities. Work with students when they have difficulty. Give them only a few pages at a time to avoid pressure.

5. **Do** a practice activity together. Review with students how to do comprehension skills.

OVERVIEW: FACTS

Introducing the Skill

Remind students that facts are things they can taste, touch, feel, smell, and see. Explain that successful readers pay close attention to details. Emphasize that the questions in the Facts unit ask about details stated in the reading selections. Students should be able to show where the answer to a question is located in a selection.

How the Lessons Are Organized

A lesson consists of a reading selection about a single topic broken into two parts. Each part is followed by five questions that require students to find restated facts from the selection.

Practice Activity

Read this story to your students.

Snakes

If you're afraid of snakes, maybe it's because you don't know much about these interesting animals. There are more than 2,700 different kinds of snakes. They live on every continent of the world except Antarctica. They come in all sizes. The largest snake ever measured was a python that was 32 feet long. One of the smallest is the thread snake, which is only about 4 inches long.

Have students answer the following questions about the story.

1. The thread snake is
   A. 4 feet long   C. 32 feet long
   B. 4 inches long   D. 32 inches long

2. The continent that has no snakes is
   A. Africa   C. Antarctica
   B. Australia   D. South America

3. The largest snake ever measured was
   A. a python   C. a thread snake
   B. a continent snake   D. an antarctic snake

Explain to students that they should look for facts while reading the stories. They should read each question carefully and try to find a sentence in the story that has some of the same words as the question.

OVERVIEW: SEQUENCE

Introducing the Skill

Remind students that when they read, the events or steps presented in a story have a special sequence. Explain that clue words, like *today, then, first, after, then,* and *finally,* can help them find what happens first, next, and last in a story. Tell students that sequence can also be implied. Finding sequence without signal words means paying careful attention to verb tense. Another clue to implied sequence is the order in which information is presented. Students need to know that writers usually relate the events in a story in order. If there are no time signals, students can assume that events have occurred in the order in which they are presented.

How the Lessons Are Organized

A lesson consists of a reading selection about a single topic, followed by five questions. The first question asks students to put statements in order based on the information in each selection. The following questions ask about the stated or implied sequence in each selection.

Practice Activity

Read this story to your students.

George Washington Carver

George Washington Carver was a famous American scientist. He was born in Missouri. Later he went to school in Iowa. Then he became a teacher at the Tuskegee Institute in Alabama. While he was teaching, he also did experiments with crops. He found hundreds of uses for peanuts, sweet potatoes, and soybeans. When he died in 1943, he was known all over the world for his discoveries. Ten years later, the home where he was born became a national monument.

Have students answer the following questions about the story.

1. Put these events in the order that they happened. What happened first, second, last?
   Carver made many discoveries. (2)
   Carver's home became a national monument. (3)
   Carver became a teacher at the Tuskegee Institute. (1)

2. When did Carver do experiments with crops?
   A. before he was in Missouri
   B. after he became famous
   C. while he was teaching

3. When did Carver's home become a national monument?
   A. when he lived in Alabama
   B. after he died
   C. while he was teaching

Explain to students that they should find words in the questions that are the same as words in the story, find time words in the story, and look at the order of the events in the story.

OVERVIEW: CONTEXT

Introducing the Skill

Review this skill with students by using a simple cloze-type procedure. Ask students to supply the missing word in "The pretty, yellow ___ swam happily in the pond." Discuss how they know the word is *fish*. Remind students to pay attention to the meaning of surrounding words and phrases. Also, have them focus on language clues such as the position of the unknown or missing word in the sentence and what kind of words come before and after it.

How the Lessons Are Organized

A lesson consists of four reading selections. In lessons 1 through 6, the selections are presented in a cloze format with one or two missing words. In lessons 7 through 12, the selections contain a word in boldface type. Students are asked to use the context of the selection to choose the correct definition for each boldfaced word.

Practice Activity

Read this story to your students.

Henry Ford built cars that everyone could buy. He cut the costs of <u>(1)</u>. He passed the savings on to his <u>(2)</u>.

1. A. chatter   <u>B. production</u>   C. sleep   D. winter

2. A. towns   B. models   <u>C. customers</u>   D. cowards

The scientists studied the volcano carefully. There was a lump on its side. The lump was getting bigger. They knew that the volcano would **erupt** soon. They warned all the people who lived nearby to move before it blew up.

3. In this paragraph, the word **erupt** means

    A. disappear   <u>C. blow up</u>
    B. get bigger   D. bring rain

Remind students that to use context, they should keep reading even if they find a word they do not know. The right answer is the word that goes with the other words in the story. If they can't find the answer the first time, they should look back at the story.

OVERVIEW: MAIN IDEA

Introducing the Skill

Have students recall a movie that they have recently seen. Ask them to state the plot of the movie using one sentence. Explain that this sentence is the main idea of the movie. Point out the difference between the main idea of the movie and the details that support the main idea. Stress that all of the details add up to the main idea.

How the Lessons Are Organized

A lesson consists of three short reading selections for which students are asked to identify the main idea. Lessons 1 through 6 have stated main ideas, while units 7 through 12 have implied main ideas.

Practice Activity

Read these paragraphs to your students.

The monarch butterfly makes a long trip south each fall. Some butterflies fly almost eighteen hundred miles from the northern United States to Mexico. As spring warms the air, the butterflies begin to return. The butterflies lay their eggs and then die. The young return to the north to start the cycle over again.

The story mainly tells
   A. which butterflies make the trip
   B. how far the insects fly
   C. when butterflies lay their eggs
   D. what the monarch's long trip is like

The front part of a newspaper contains important stories of national and local events. The sports pages report scores and give information about players, coaches, and teams. The comics section makes many people laugh.

The story mainly tells
   A. what the front section contains
   B. where you can read about players
   C. about different parts of a newspaper
   D. what makes people laugh

For Lessons 1-6, have students read the whole story. Then have students ask themselves, "Which sentence is the sum of all the other sentences?" Explain that it will be the main idea.

For Lessons 7-12, have students read the whole story. Then they should figure out what the details have in common. Tell them to think about what the writer is trying to tell them.

OVERVIEW: CONCLUSION

Introducing the Skill

Emphasize that practicing this skill means thinking about what is actually stated in the reading selection. Ask students what they can conclude from the sentence, "Sylvia rushed into the kitchen and yanked the cookies from the smoking oven." Students can conclude that Sylvia was not in the kitchen before she pulled the cookies out of the oven. Point out that the sentence states that "Sylvia rushed into the kitchen." Students cannot conclude that Sylvia was baking the cookies, although they could infer this, because the sentence gives no evidence to support that conclusion. Perhaps another family member or friend was baking the cookies. Remind students that the conclusion they draw must be supported by the information in the selection in order to be a correct, or logical, conclusion.

How the Lessons Are Organized

Each lesson contains three short reading selections for which students are asked to choose a conclusion that can logically be drawn from the information presented. Lessons 7 through 12 are more difficult because students are asked to identify a conclusion that cannot be drawn from the information presented.

Practice Activity

Read this paragraph to your students.

Crocodiles sometimes eat other crocodiles—even their own young. They attack and eat large land animals, such as water buffalo, that come to the swamp to drink water. Crocodiles hold their victims underwater until they drown.

From the story you can tell that

A. crocodiles attack only when they are scared
B. crocodiles are very particular about what they eat
C. crocodiles have very strong jaws
D. people shouldn't be afraid of crocodiles

Remind students to read all the clues in the story. They should find a conclusion that fits all the clues. To make sure that they find the correct conclusion, they should ask, "How do I know this?" They should know because of the clues in the story.

OVERVIEW: INFERENCE

Introducing the Skill

Have students imagine that they are at a friend's house. Tell them there is a cake with candles on one table and many presents on another. Balloons and crepe-paper streamers hang from the ceiling. There are many people there. Ask students to make an inference about why this is a special day for their friend. Discuss what facts and personal knowledge or experiences lead them to infer that their friend is having a birthday party. Remind students that they can make inferences by thinking about what they already know and adding it to the facts given in the reading selection. Point out that facts can be found in the selection but that the inference cannot.

How the Lessons Are Organized

A lesson consists of three short reading selections. Factual and inferential statements follow each reading selection. Students must differentiate the facts in the selection from the inferences that can logically be made.

Practice Activity

Read this story to your students.

Laura had $5.00. Her mother had given the money to her so that she could buy a birthday present for her brother. While Laura was shopping, she saw a book she had been wanting to read. It cost $4.50.

Fact   Inference

Fact	Inference	
○	○	**A.** Laura had $5.00. (F)
○	○	**B.** The book cost $4.50. (F)
○	○	**C.** Laura bought the book she wanted. (I)
○	○	**D.** She didn't have a present to give to her brother. (I)

Remind students to keep in mind the difference between facts and inferences. They should think about the facts in the story and what they already know. Encourage them to make an inference by putting together what they know and what they read.

Dear Parent:

During this school year, our class will be working on a variety of reading skills. We will be completing activity sheets that provide practice in the comprehension skills that can help your child become a better reader. The skills we will be focusing on are: finding the facts, detecting a sequence, learning new vocabulary through context, identifying the main idea, drawing conclusions, and making inferences.

From time to time, I may send home activity sheets. To best help your child, please consider the following suggestions:

- Provide a quiet place to work.
- Go over the directions together.
- Encourage your child to do his or her best.
- Check the lesson when it is complete.
- Go over your child's work, and note improvements as well as problems.

Help your child maintain a positive attitude about reading. Provide as many opportunities for reading with your child as possible. Read books from the library, comics in the newspaper, even cereal boxes. Let your child know that each lesson provides an opportunity to have fun and to learn. Above all, enjoy this time you spend with your child. He or she will feel your support, and skills will improve with each activity completed.

Thank you for your help!

Cordially,

Name _____   Date _____

Hug Someone Else, Please!

Read the story. Choose the answer that best completes each sentence.

Many people think that an octopus makes a curious sight. It has eight arms coming out of a rounded head. Its name, *octopus*, comes from two Greek words that mean "eight feet."

People once thought that the octopus was a "devilfish" or a "monster of the sea." They thought that an octopus had arms long enough to hug a whole ship. But experts today know that this is not true. These odd sea creatures actually prefer to be left alone. And even the largest type of octopus is too small to hug a ship. Their average length is only about ten feet. Most kinds are not any larger than a person's fist. However, an octopus that feels threatened *will* bite, using its sharp, parrot-like beak. Also, every once in a while, an octopus will "hug" a diver.

_____ **1.** An octopus has
  A. six arms   C. eight arms
  B. four arms   D. two arms

_____ **2.** People once thought that the octopus was a
  A. mammal   C. whale
  B. monster   D. pet

_____ **3.** The octopus likes to
  A. be left alone   C. attack people
  B. play with people D. swim beside boats

_____ **4.** The average length of an octopus is
  A. twelve feet   C. ten feet
  B. thirty feet   D. fifty feet

_____ **5.** Octopuses have parrot-like
  A. wings   C. eyes
  B. beaks   D. tails

Go on to the next page.

Name _____   Date _____

Even though it cannot pull ships under the sea, an octopus can use its arms to move rocks much heavier than itself. Its arms can also handle tiny objects quite well. In one study scientists placed food in screw-top jars for an octopus. The octopus unscrewed the lid and then ate the food from the jar.

An octopus uses its arms mainly to gather food. It eats shellfish, including clams, crabs, and lobsters. It leaves its den at the bottom of the sea at night. When an octopus finds a crab or something else good to eat, it releases poison into the water. This makes the victim easy to catch. For the trip home, the octopus gathers the food into the skin between its arms. This area is called the web. When its web is full, the octopus returns home for a fine meal.

_____ **6.** An octopus will use its arms to
    A. pull ships down   **C.** poison a crab
    B. attack people   **D.** move large objects

_____ **7.** When given a screw-top jar, an octopus will probably
    A. break it   **C.** swallow it
    B. open it   **D.** look at it

_____ **8.** An octopus uses its arms mainly to
    A. eat   **C.** move rocks
    B. fight   **D.** carry young

_____ **9.** The octopus carries its food in
    A. its mouth   **C.** a layer of skin
    B. its beak   **D.** its arms

_____ **10.** The octopus eats its meals
    A. above its den **C.** away from home
    B. in its den   **D.** while swimming

Comprehension 6, SV 6188-5

Name _____   Date _____

Cats in History

Read the story. Choose the answer that best completes each sentence.

Cats first became pets long, long ago. This may have happened as early as 3500 B.C. People in early Egypt loved cats. The cats kept homes free of rats, mice, and snakes. Cats also kept pests away from farms and places where grain was stored.

A thousand years later, cats in Egypt had become more important than ever. They were protected by law. Under the law, people who harmed cats could be put to death. Also during this time, cat owners had a special way to express their sadness when a pet cat died. The owners shaved their eyebrows to show how much they had loved their special pet. Cats even became part of the religion in certain areas of Egypt. In those places people prayed to a goddess of love named Bast. Statues of Bast had a cat's head and a woman's body.

_____ **1.** Cats became pets as early as
   A. 1000 B.C.   C. 3500 B.C.
   B. 2000 B.C.   D. 5000 B.C.

_____ **2.** Cats in early Egypt kept pests away from
   A. farms   C. streets
   B. rats   D. trees

_____ **3.** People who harmed cats were sometimes
   A. put in jail   C. given honors
   B. cheered   D. put to death

_____ **4.** When people's cats died, they shaved their
   A. heads   C. arms
   B. eyebrows   D. beards

_____ **5.** Bast had a cat's
   A. legs   C. body
   B. fur   D. head

Go on to the next page.

Name _____   Date _____

People in the Far East also loved cats. They used cats to keep mice from nibbling holy books in temples. Cats also kept mice from eating silkworm cocoons. Silk makers traded silk cloth for other fine goods, so they depended on their cats.

Cats in Europe in the 1300s were not treated as well. People killed them by the thousands because they were a symbol of bad luck. This caused the number of rats to grow. Rats carried diseases. A deadly disease called black death spread, killing one fourth of all people in Europe.

Over time people once again learned that cats keep many pests away. By the 1600s cats had again become popular. Settlers arriving in the New World brought cats with them. Some of the cats you know today came from those early cats.

_____ **6.** Cats in the Far East kept mice away from
    A. water   **C.** cocoons
    B. people   **D.** Europe

_____ **7.** People in Europe in the 1300s thought cats were
    A. cute   **C.** good
    B. fun   **D.** bad

_____ **8.** With fewer cats the number of rats
    A. was larger   **C.** stayed the same
    B. was smaller   **D.** was unimportant

_____ **9.** One fourth of the people in Europe
    A. moved   **C.** owned cats
    B. died   **D.** loved cats

_____ **10.** By the 1600s people once again
    A. liked cats   **C.** killed cats
    B. saved rats   **D.** hated cats

Name _____   Date _____

Showboats

Read the story. Choose the answer that best completes each sentence.

In pioneer days the coming of a showboat was a big event. It was the only fun for many settlers along the Mississippi and Ohio rivers. There were no movies. A boat bringing singers, dancers, and actors was a big treat.

One of the first groups to perform from a boat was the Chapman family. They floated from town to town on a large, flat boat. The boat was one hundred feet long. After they landed, the Chapmans paraded through the town. They played trumpets and hung posters to announce their show. That night almost everyone in town came to see them.

Tickets cost fifty cents. But instead of paying money, some people traded things they had grown or made. The Chapmans often got fresh berries or homemade bread!

_____ 1. For many settlers the showboat was their only
    A. radio   C. appearance
    B. parade   D. entertainment

_____ 2. In pioneer days there were no
    A. boats   C. trumpets
    B. movies   D. plays

_____ 3. The Chapman family floated from
    A. town to town   C. stage to stage
    B. boat to boat   D. across the ocean

_____ 4. Tickets cost
    A. five cents   C. one hundred boats
    B. fifty cents   D. fifty berries

_____ 5. Instead of paying money for tickets, some people
    A. traded things C. trained actors
    B. performed acts D. tricked others

Go on to the next page.

Name _____   Date _____

In 1836 the Chapmans bought a steamboat. The steamboat had its own power, so it could go against the flow of the rivers. The Chapmans could visit many more towns.

Soon other showboats were on the rivers, too. Some of the most popular boats had circuses on them. One huge boat was called the *Floating Circus Palace*. It was built in 1851. The *Palace* was big enough to carry forty horses. More than three thousand people at a time could watch a show on the *Palace*.

Gradually people began to move west. The little towns along the rivers grew to be big cities. The people built their own theaters and circuses. Movies were invented. When a showboat arrived, only a few people came to greet it. The last great showboat to float on the rivers was the *Golden Rod*. It stopped giving shows in 1943.

_____ **6.** The Chapmans bought a steamboat in
     A. 1863   C. 1851
     B. 1836   D. 1943

_____ **7.** The steamboat made it easier to visit more
     A. communities   C. acrobats
     B. fairs   D. currents

_____ **8.** Some of the most popular boats carried
     A. famous people   C. circus performers
     B. floating zoos   D. television crews

_____ **9.** The *Floating Circus Palace* was
     A. small   C. light
     B. last   D. large

_____ **10.** The *Palace* could hold more than three thousand
     A. theaters   C. customers
     B. horses   D. countries

Name _____   Date _____

The Greatest

Read the story. Choose the answer that best completes each sentence.

At age 18 Mildred Ella Didrikson was already on her way to becoming the greatest woman athlete in history. She loved to play baseball. She was nicknamed "Babe" after Babe Ruth, the famous baseball player. She grew up in Beaumont, Texas. In high school Babe was the star of the basketball team. She was also the All-City Champion high diver. She played baseball, football, pool, and tennis. She boxed and swam. In track and field, she won contest after contest. Then she moved to Dallas. There she became the All-American Girls Basketball Champion.

There was only one place left for her to test her skills. At the 1932 Olympic games, the crowd watched in excitement as Babe set new world records. She threw the javelin more than 143 feet. She ran the women's 80-meter hurdles in under 12 seconds. Babe proudly accepted two gold medals.

_____ **1.** Mildred Ella Didrikson was
  A. from Canada   **C.** a great athlete
  B. a movie star   **D.** a famous writer

_____ **2.** Mildred Ella's nickname, "Babe," comes from
  A. a baseball star   **C.** her friend Sue Ellen
  B. a book she read   **D.** a basketball champion

_____ **3.** Babe was the best high diver in
  A. track   **C.** the Olympics
  B. Beaumont   **D.** Dallas

_____ **4.** Babe threw the javelin more than
  A. 12 seconds   **C.** 180 feet
  B. 80 meters   **D.** 143 feet

_____ **5.** At the 1932 Olympics, Babe
  A. hurt her arm   **C.** won two gold medals
  B. played baseball   **D.** worked in the field

Go on to the next page.

Name _____   Date _____

When the Olympics were over, a man named Grantland Rice talked to Babe. Rice was a famous sportswriter. He suggested to Babe that she try a sport that was new to her. He wanted her to play golf! "Well, I'll try it," said Babe, "just for the fun of it." As it turned out, Babe spent most of the rest of her life playing golf. By the time she was 24, she was already a champion player. During one golf tournament, Babe met George Zaharias. They liked one another right away and soon got married. George began managing Babe's career.

Babe became seriously ill with cancer. But the cancer operation didn't stop her from playing golf. She kept winning, and she donated most of her prize money to the American Cancer Society. The disease spread, however. Babe died in Galveston, Texas, in 1956.

_____

_____ **6.** Babe tried a new sport after she talked to a
     A. writer   C. golfer
     B. winner   D. runner

_____ **7.** Babe met George Zaharias
     A. at the Olympics   C. at a golf contest
     B. in a hospital   D. at a business meeting

_____ **8.** George was Babe's
     A. writer   C. trainer
     B. manager   D. athlete

_____ **9.** After her operation, Babe
     A. started writing   C. gave up sports
     B. went home   D. kept playing golf

_____ **10.** Babe gave the American Cancer Society
     A. golf   C. trouble
     B. sports   D. money

Name _____ Date _____

Music for Less

Read the story. Choose the answer that best completes each sentence.

Music recordings are very expensive these days. But there are many ways to save. One way you can get music for less is to borrow records and tapes from a library. But remember to return the library tapes and records when they are due. If you don't, you'll have to pay a fine. Then the music won't be free.

You can also get free music by using swaps or exchanges. Many music stores have a wall chart with information about trading recordings. People list the records and tapes they want to trade. After the title they write *good*, *fair*, or *poor* to let you know the condition of the recording. People have to be honest for this to work.

If you have a blank tape, you can make a copy of a friend's record. Record companies don't like for people to do this. They don't make as much money. But it's not against the law, as long as you do not sell your copy.

_____ 1. You can borrow records and tapes from
    A. a library   C. the record exchange
    B. a record store   D. a record company

_____ 2. Record and tape exchange information is
for people who
    A. spend money   C. trade music
    B. go to libraries   D. have blank tapes

_____ 3. The words *good* or *poor* let you know a record's
    A. popularity   C. owner
    B. condition   D. title

_____ 4. Record companies don't like for people to
    A. pay fines   C. buy tapes
    B. own records   D. copy records

_____ 5. You are not allowed to record music on tape and
    A. use it   C. sell it
    B. swap it   D. share it

Go on to the next page.

Name _____   Date _____

If you have some money to spend on music, you don't have to pay the list price. *List price* is the price that the record company suggests to the music store. Wait for a sale. Sale prices are below list price.

Many music lovers go to yard sales, garage sales, and stores that sell used records. In these places you have to look through stacks and stacks of old records. Usually they aren't sorted. You have to take your time. You might not find anything that interests you at all. But sometimes you'll find a real treasure! You could find a rare record made long ago. You might discover something by a group that is no longer together.

A patient person can build a fine music collection. It doesn't have to take a lot of money. But it does take a lot of time.

_____ **6.** The list price is set by the record
    A. store   **C.** sale
    B. company   **D.** money

_____ **7.** In a sale, records are
    A. better   **C.** higher
    B. cheaper   **D.** older

_____ **8.** Records at a garage sale are usually
    A. new   **C.** in order
    B. expensive   **D.** in stacks

_____ **9.** If you're lucky, you may find a used record that is
    A. broken   **C.** expensive
    B. overdue   **D.** rare

_____ **10.** Building a collection takes a lot of
    A. time   **C.** good shape
    B. new hits   **D.** money

Name _____   Date _____

At the Ends of the Earth

Read the story. Choose the answer that best completes each sentence.

Do you think that the North Pole and the South Pole are alike? Most people do. But in fact the two areas are quite different. The North Pole is in the Arctic Ocean. The South Pole lies near the center of Antarctica. Antarctica is colder than the Arctic. In fact, Antarctica is by far the coldest region on Earth.

One reason for Antarctica's very cold climate is that it has mountains high above sea level. Summers there rarely get above freezing. Ice and snow cover almost all of Antarctica throughout the entire year.

The Arctic region includes lands around the Arctic Ocean. The Arctic region is mostly at or near sea level. In parts of the Arctic, summers can be as warm as those in Boston. They just do not last as long. Most of the Arctic lands have no snow or ice in the summer.

_____ **1.** The North Pole is
   A. on land   **C.** in the Arctic Ocean
   B. on a mountain   **D.** in Antarctica

_____ **2.** Antarctica is the coldest
   A. region   **C.** city
   B. state   **D.** nation

_____ **3.** Antarctica has
   A. rivers   **C.** mountains
   B. sand   **D.** jungles

_____ **4.** The Arctic is the area around
   A. Boston   **C.** the South Pole
   B. Antarctica   **D.** the North Pole

_____ **5.** The Arctic is mostly
   A. in Boston   **C.** above sea level
   B. at sea level   **D.** below sea level

Go on to the next page.

Name _____   Date _____

Antarctica also has most of the world's permanent ice. The ice rests on land. Its average thickness is 8,000 feet. But ice in the Arctic rests on water. Its thickness varies from 10 to 65 feet.

If you traveled to the Arctic, you would see reindeer, polar bears, seals, birds, and insects. If your stay lasted through all the seasons, you might see over a thousand types of plants. You might also meet some of the people who live there. These people have learned to live in the cold climate quite well. They have been able to use the plants and animals there. Most of the people live near the sea, where they catch fish.

If you visited Antarctica, you would see ice and more ice. Very few animals and plants can live there. Most animals live on the coast. The largest animal that can live on the mainland is a small fly. And you would not see people at all, unless you ran into an explorer or a scientist.

_____

_____ **6.** In the Arctic, ice rests on
    A. ice   **C.** land
    B. plants   **D.** the ocean

_____ **7.** Compared to ice in the Arctic, ice in Antarctica is
    A. whiter   **C.** thicker
    B. smaller   **D.** thinner

_____ **8.** In the Arctic, you would see
    A. only ice   **C.** no animals
    B. no plants   **D.** many animals

_____ **9.** The largest animal on mainland Antarctica is a
    A. fly   **C.** polar bear
    B. fish   **D.** reindeer

_____ **10.** If you saw people in Antarctica, they might be
    A. farmers   **C.** digging up trees
    B. scientists   **D.** hunting reindeer

Name _____   Date _____

The Eyes Have It

Read the story. Choose the answer that best completes each sentence.

Try an experiment. Hold your arms out to your sides. Extend your index fingers and slowly bring your arms together in front of you. Try to make your fingers touch. Since that was so easy, try it again with only one eye open.

If you are like most people, the task is more challenging using only one eye. There is a reason for this. A certain signal goes to your brain when you look at objects with both eyes. This signal tells your brain how close or how far away objects are. If you use only one eye, your brain does not receive this signal. You cannot judge distance correctly or tell how thick objects are. You have lost your ability to see depth. When you look at objects with one eye, your brain "sees" the scene as if it were painted on a flat screen. Using two eyes gives depth to the same view.

_____

_____ 1. You begin the experiment by holding your arms
   A. behind you   C. out to your sides
   B. above your head   D. down by your sides

_____ 2. Next you bring your arms
   A. down   C. behind your head
   B. up   D. in front of you

_____ 3. It is easiest to make your fingers meet if you have
   A. good luck   C. one eye closed
   B. good vision   D. both eyes open

_____ 4. To judge distance, use
   A. one eye   C. your arms
   B. both eyes   D. your fingers

_____ 5. When you use one eye, the brain "sees"
   A. a flat scene   C. only large things
   B. far away   D. only small things

Go on to the next page.

Comprehension 6, SV 6188-5

Name _____ Date _____

Each of your eyes sees things from a slightly different angle. Your left eye sees more of the objects to your left, and your right eye sees more of the objects to your right. Try another experiment. Look at a nearby object with one eye closed, and notice what you can see. Then close the other eye and look at the same object. How does this change what you see? Now look with both eyes. When you have both eyes open, each eye sees not only the front of the object but also a little on each side.

This special vision is called depth perception. Depth perception makes you able to judge distances. It helps you avoid running into things. It helps you catch a ball. Newborn babies do not have this ability. It takes a few years for it to develop. That is why some children who have trouble in sports become wonderful athletes later.

_____ **6.** Each of your eyes sees things from a different
  A. angle   **C.** signal
  B. nerve   **D.** light

_____ **7.** Your left eye sees more of the objects
  A. to the left   **C.** to the center
  B. to the right   **D.** to the front

_____ **8.** When both your eyes are open, they
  A. work less   **C.** stand apart
  B. see more   **D.** work harder

_____ **9.** Depth perception makes you able to judge
  A. angles   **C.** eyes
  B. color   **D.** distances

_____ **10.** Depth perception is well developed in
  A. children   **C.** athletes
  B. newborns   **D.** objects

Name _____   Date _____

Remarkable Journey

How does a young dog or cat get to know a new home? The animal uses its nose. Right away it sniffs its new surroundings. Then it makes wider and wider circles, sniffing all the time. Before long it can find its way home very well, even in the dark. It simply follows familiar scents.

But stories exist of animals who found their way across land they had never "sniffed" before. Take the case of Smoky, the Persian cat. Smoky had a funny tuft of red fur under his chin. One day Smoky and his owner began a long journey. They were moving from Oklahoma to Tennessee. When they were just 18 miles from their Oklahoma home, Smoky jumped out of the car. Somehow he found his way back to the old house. There he wandered around outside for many days. Finally he disappeared.

A year later Smoky meowed at the door of a house in Tennessee. A man opened the door. "Is that you, Smoky?" he whispered. At first he couldn't believe it. Then he recognized the tuft of red fur. It was Smoky!

A dog named Bobby also made a remarkable journey. Bobby lived at a farmhouse in a small town in France. One day Bobby's master decided to take him to Paris, 35 miles away. For hours the two wandered through the crowded, noisy city. At the end of the day, when it was time to go home, Bobby's master looked down. The dog had disappeared! The man searched everywhere, but he finally decided that his dog was gone forever, and he sadly went home. Five days later Bobby was barking at the farmhouse door!

Perhaps the most amazing journey of all was made by Prince, a dog who belonged to a British soldier. During World War I, Prince's master was sent to France to fight. After his master left, Prince somehow crossed a wide body of water called the English Channel. Remarkably the dog managed to find his master in the trench where he was fighting.

Go on to the next page.

Name _____   Date _____

1. Put these events in the order that they happened. What happened first? Write the number **1** on the line by that sentence. Then write the number **2** by the sentence that tells what happened next. Write the number **3** by the sentence that tells what happened last.

_____ Smoky traveled to Tennessee.

_____ Smoky jumped out of the car.

_____ Smoky went to his old home.

Choose the phrase that best answers each question.

_____ 2. What is the first thing a pet does in a new place?
    A. travels long distances
    B. explores its surroundings
    C. finds its way in the dark

_____ 3. When was the man sure the cat was Smoky?
    A. when he saw the tuft of fur
    B. as soon as he opened the door
    C. before he opened the door

_____ 4. When did the man discover that Bobby was gone?
    A. after 35 miles
    B. five days later
    C. at the end of the day

_____ 5. What did Prince do just before he found his master?
    A. found the British Army
    B. crossed the English Channel
    C. located a trench

Name _____   Date _____

Pioneer Pilot

In 1926 the aviation industry was just getting started. Only six thousand Americans flew as passengers in planes that year. Most people still thought that flying was just a fast and dangerous sport.

But not everyone thought flying was for the birds. A young woman named Edna Gardner Whyte thought it was important. She thought people would travel by plane in the future. In 1926 Whyte was learning to be a pilot. Most of her teachers told her to quit. They said flying a plane was no job for a woman. But Edna Whyte didn't listen. She went on and got her pilot's license. In fact she got the best score on the test.

This didn't solve all of Edna's problems, though. Most of the airlines did not want a woman for a pilot. Even though she was a good pilot, she couldn't get a job flying planes. She had to keep proving herself again and again. In 1934 she entered a flying race in Maryland. The other pilots laughed at her. They were all men. They didn't laugh when Edna won the race, though. The next year the same race took place. This time a sign said *Men Only*.

Edna went right on flying and winning. In 1937 she won another race. Amelia Earhart handed her the prize. Earhart was also a great pilot. She was the first woman to fly alone across the Atlantic Ocean. Amelia was famous. But Edna Whyte had flown many more hours than Earhart.

Sadly, Earhart disappeared on a flight in 1937. No one ever found her or her plane. But Whyte went on flying until she was in her eighties. She put in more than thirty thousand hours in the air. When she quit racing, she became a teacher. She taught many other people to fly. Her favorite students were young women.

Go on to the next page.

Name _____   Date _____

1. Put these events in the order that they happened. What happened first? Write the number **1** on the line by that sentence. Then write the number **2** by the sentence that tells what happened next. Write the number **3** by the sentence that tells what happened last.

_____ Edna Gardner Whyte won a race.

_____ Edna Gardner Whyte learned to fly.

_____ Edna Gardner Whyte got her pilot's license.

Choose the phrase that best answers each question.

_____ 2. When did teachers tell Edna to quit?
    A. before she took flying lessons
    B. after she taught others
    C. while she was learning to fly

_____ 3. When did the *Men Only* sign go up in Maryland?
    A. in 1934
    B. in 1935
    C. in 1926

_____ 4. When did Amelia Earhart disappear?
    A. after she gave Edna Whyte a trophy
    B. at the time she gave Edna Whyte a trophy
    C. before she gave Edna Whyte a trophy

_____ 5. When did Whyte become a flying teacher?
    A. at the end of her career
    B. at the beginning of her career
    C. before she got her pilot's license

Name _____   Date _____

Chief Joseph

The Nez Percé are a tribe of Native Americans. They once lived in Oregon, Washington, and Idaho. They lived near the rivers and fished for salmon. In 1840 a young man named Joseph was born. When he grew up, he became Chief Joseph. During this time more and more white settlers moved to his land.

The Nez Percé wanted to live in peace with the settlers. In 1855 they signed a treaty with the United States government. The tribe agreed to give up part of their land and live on a reservation in Oregon.

But in 1860 gold was discovered on the reservation. Gold miners and settlers moved onto the land. In May of 1877, the government ordered all the Nez Percé to move to another reservation, far away in Idaho. The tribe was angry. They didn't want to leave the land of their ancestors.

Some of the chiefs wanted to go to war. But Chief Joseph knew they could not win. He convinced the tribe to travel east. By June 13 they were near the new reservation. Several angry warriors left camp and killed 18 settlers. This act started a war.

For four months the Nez Percé fought and hid in mountains and canyons. They decided to go to Canada, for there the army could not follow them. The tribe stopped to rest near the Bear Paw Mountains in Montana. They were only thirty miles from Canada.

But there the army surrounded the Nez Percé. The tribe fought bravely for five days. But it was winter, and they had no blankets or food. The children were freezing to death. On October 5, 1877, Chief Joseph surrendered.

Go on to the next page.

Name _____   Date _____

1. Put these events in the order that they happened. What happened first? Write the number **1** on the line by that sentence. Then write the number **2** by the sentence that tells what happened next. Write the number **3** by the sentence that tells what happened last.

_____ The Nez Percé traveled toward Canada.

_____ Several angry warriors killed 18 settlers.

_____ The government ordered the Nez Percé to move.

Choose the phrase that best answers each question.

_____ **2.** When did the Nez Percé agree to live on a reservation in Oregon?
   A. after Chief Joseph surrendered
   B. when a treaty was signed
   C. after the Nez Percé fought the army

_____ **3.** When was gold discovered on the reservation?
   A. in 1860
   B. when a Nez Percé boy was fishing for salmon
   C. during the summer of 1877

_____ **4.** When were the Nez Percé ordered to move to Idaho?
   A. before the treaty of 1855 was signed
   B. after the 18 settlers were killed
   C. after gold was discovered

_____ **5.** When did Chief Joseph surrender?
   A. after fighting for five days in Montana
   B. while they were in Oregon
   C. on June 13, 1877

Name _____   Date _____

Benjamin Banneker

Benjamin Banneker was born in 1731 near Baltimore. He became the best-known African American of his time. When Benjamin started school he loved it, especially math and science. But his father needed more help around the farm. One day he told Benjamin that he would have to quit school.

Benjamin wanted to continue learning. He decided that he would study on his own. He borrowed books and stayed up late every night reading and doing math problems.

When Benjamin was 22, a merchant loaned him a pocket watch. Benjamin was fascinated! He had heard of clocks but had never seen one. He took the back off and made sketches of the gears. Benjamin decided that he would make his own clock. Carefully he carved the gears out of wood. He studied his sketches and made each part exactly right. The clock kept perfect time for 45 years!

Next Benjamin became interested in the night sky. He noticed that the stars moved. Was there a pattern to this movement? He decided to find out. Each night he sat outside and observed the sky. He made sketches and charts and taught himself astronomy.

The more Benjamin learned, the more he wanted to learn. In 1783, when he was 52, he sold the family farm. Now at last he was able to devote all his time to learning. He taught himself the skill of surveying. In 1791 he helped survey the nation's new capital city, Washington, D. C. That same year he began publishing an almanac. This book predicted the weather and told about the tides. Benjamin printed the almanac for ten years. In spite of his difficult circumstances, Benjamin had followed his dreams. His talent and self-discipline had made it possible for him to accomplish his many goals.

Go on to the next page.

Name _____   Date _____

1. Put these events in the order that they happened. What happened first? Write the number **1** on the line by that sentence. Then write the number **2** by the sentence that tells what happened next. Write the number **3** by the sentence that tells what happened last.

_____ Benjamin sold the family farm.

_____ Benjamin went to school.

_____ Benjamin made a clock based on his sketches.

Choose the phrase that best answers each question.

_____ **2.** When did Benjamin first see a watch?

    A. after he wrote the almanac

    B. when he was 22

    C. when he first went to school

_____ **3.** When did Benjamin teach himself astronomy?

    A. before he made the clock

    B. while he was in school

    C. before he sold the family farm

_____ **4.** When did Benjamin sell the family farm?

    A. before he quit school

    B. before he made the watch

    C. before he learned surveying

_____ **5.** When did Benjamin first publish his almanac?

    A. before he made the clock

    B. in 1791

    C. when he was 22

Name _____   Date _____

Safe Milk

Today we know the milk we buy is safe to drink. But this wasn't always so. In the 1800s many diseases were spread by germs in milk. At last a way to kill these germs was found. But it took years for this process to be accepted. And it might have taken much longer if it hadn't been for Nathan Straus.

Nathan Straus and his brother Isidor were businessmen in New York City. They owned Macy's Department Store. Nathan Straus had read about Louis Pasteur. Pasteur had developed a way of heating milk to kill germs that cause disease. His method was called pasteurization. Straus became convinced that all milk should be pasteurized. His fight to convince others took twenty years.

In 1891 the first pasteurizer was put in a milk plant in the United States. But some people fought this idea. Dairy farmers didn't want to buy the machine. Other people didn't think it was necessary. They thought keeping cows clean was enough to make milk safe.

In New York City, one child in ten died before the age of five. Straus was convinced that bad milk was one of the causes. He wanted to help. In 1893 he set up a stand and sold pasteurized milk in a poor neighborhood. He sold the milk for a low price. Many people bought milk there. The young children in the neighborhood became healthier. Few of them died. In the next few years, Straus set up 12 more stands.

In 1907 Straus and others wanted a law passed that would force milk producers to pasteurize milk. But those who sold milk were against the law. It was voted down. Straus kept fighting. He gave speeches, wrote letters, and spoke to the city leaders. Finally pasteurization was accepted. By 1914, 95 percent of New York City's milk supply was pasteurized. The death rate of young children dropped almost at once. In 1923 Straus was given an award for his efforts to help the people of New York City.

Go on to the next page.

Name _____   Date _____

1. Put these events in the order that they happened. What happened first?
Write the number **1** on the line by that sentence. Then write the number **2** by
the sentence that tells what happened next. Write the number **3** by the sentence
that tells what happened last.

_____ Straus wanted to stop the sale of unsafe milk.

_____ Louis Pasteur found a way to kill the germs in milk.

_____ Straus was given an award for his public service.

Choose the phrase that best answers each question.

_____ **2.** When were many diseases spread by milk?

    A. after Straus received his award

    B. before pasteurization was accepted

    C. in 1914

_____ **3.** When was pasteurization developed?

    A. after the child death rate went down

    B. after Straus spoke to the city leaders

    C. before Straus started selling milk

_____ **4.** When did Straus set up his first milk stand?

    A. after the first pasteurizer was used in America

    B. before he owned Macy's

    C. after he was given a public-service award

_____ **5.** When did the child death rate drop?

    A. before Straus fought for pasteurization

    B. soon after most of the city's milk was pasteurized

    C. in 1891

Name _____   Date _____

Yellowstone Park on Fire!

1988 is a year that will not be forgotten for a long time at Yellowstone National Park. Fires broke out in June and burned fiercely until September. The flames were not put out completely until November. They covered almost half of the huge park. What caused such huge fires? There are several answers to this question.

Lodgepole pines make up eighty percent of the park's forests. These trees grow quickly. But they only live about two hundred years. Then many of the pines die and are blown down by high winds. The trees lie on the forest floor for many years. In wet forests they would rot and turn back into soil. But it is too dry for this to happen in Yellowstone. In 1988 dead wood covered the forest floor.

Yellowstone usually gets a lot of snow in the winter. When the snow melts, it provides water for the plants. But for six winters in the 1980s, little snow had fallen. Rain also usually falls during the summer months. But 1988 was the driest summer in 116 years.

Several fires started in and near the park in June. Park officials fought the fires caused by human carelessness. But they didn't try to put out the fires started by lightning. They knew that fires help clean out the dead wood. But when little rain fell in June and July, the fires became larger and larger. Over 17,000 acres had burned by July 21. Park officials decided that it was time to fight the roaring fires.

On June 23 strong winds blew the fires into new areas of the park. Firefighters battled the blazes. But they had little success. On August 20 eighty mile-per-hour winds swept through the park. This day became known as Black Saturday. Fires that had almost died out came back to life. No matter how hard the firefighters tried, they couldn't control the flames. But snow and rain began to fall in September. Then the worst of the fires were put out. The remaining fires were put out by heavy snows in November.

Go on to the next page.

35

Name _____ Date _____

1. Put these events in the order that they happened. What happened first? Write the number **1** on the line by that sentence. Then write the number **2** by the sentence that tells what happened next. Write the number **3** by the sentence that tells what happened last.

_____ Yellowstone had the driest summer in 116 years.

_____ The worst of the fires were put out.

_____ Several fires started in the park.

Choose the phrase that best answers each question.

_____ **2.** When did the fires begin in Yellowstone?
    A. after many trees had died
    B. when the heavy snows fell
    C. after the strong winds blew in

_____ **3.** When did little snow fall in the park?
    A. during the 1980s
    B. in November
    C. 116 years ago

_____ **4.** When did park officials decide to fight the fires?
    A. when lightning struck
    B. after 17,000 acres had burned
    C. on Black Saturday

_____ **5.** When was Black Saturday?
    A. when the trees died
    B. one month before the first fires started
    C. when strong winds hit the park

Name _____   Date _____

Dolphins

For centuries dolphins have been thought of as special animals. Plutarch, a Greek writer, praised their friendliness two thousand years ago. Scenes of people riding on dolphins have appeared in the art of many countries.

There are more than 38 kinds of dolphins. Most types live in the ocean. They are related to whales. Dolphins are very smart. They can learn, remember, and solve problems. They are born entertainers who love to perform. You can see them do tricks at marine amusement parks.

Dolphins travel in herds. They are social animals who like to play. They often toss seaweed and driftwood up in the air. Dolphins become very unhappy and lonely if they are separated from their companions. Dolphins mate in the spring. A baby is born a year later. The other dolphins surround the mother while she is giving birth. They do this to protect her from danger. Soon after birth the mother pushes the baby to the surface so that it can breathe. The baby nurses, or drinks the mother's milk, for about 18 months. The mother teaches the baby and protects it from harm.

Many tales have been told of dolphins helping people. One famous dolphin was named Pelorus Jack. Jack lived in Cook's Strait between the North Island and South Island of New Zealand. From 1888 until the 1920s, Jack guided ships through Cook's Strait. People came from around the world to see him.

In 1978 a small fishing boat was lost off the coast of South Africa. It was caught in a thick fog and dangerous water. The fishermen told of four dolphins who led their boat to shore. Another newspaper account told of a ship that exploded. A woman was injured and thrown overboard. She said three dolphins swam near her and helped her float. They stayed with her until she could climb on a buoy. There are many other stories of dolphins saving drowning people by pushing them to shallow water.

Go on to the next page.

Comprehension 6, SV 6188-5

Name _____   Date _____

1. Put these events in the order that they happened. What happened first?
Write the number **1** on the line by that sentence. Then write the number **2** by
the sentence that tells what happened next. Write the number **3** by the sentence
that tells what happened last.

_____ The baby nurses for about 18 months.

_____ The mother pushes the baby to the surface.

_____ The other dolphins surround the mother.

Choose the phrase that best answers each question.

_____ 2. When did Plutarch praise dolphins?
    A. three hundred years ago
    B. in 1888
    C. two thousand years ago

_____ 3. When do other dolphins surround a mother dolphin?
    A. while the mother dolphin gives birth
    B. after the mother nurses her baby
    C. after the mother pushes her baby to the surface

_____ 4. When did Pelorus Jack guide ships through Cook's Strait?
    A. before Plutarch died
    B. before four dolphins helped some lost fishermen
    C. before dolphins were thought of as special animals

_____ 5. When was a small fishing boat lost off the coast of South Africa?
    A. during the time when Pelorus Jack guided ships
    B. when a woman's ship exploded
    C. in 1978

Name _____   Date _____

Read the story. Choose the answer that best completes each sentence.

The great blue whale is bigger than the dinosaurs were. A human being could stand up straight inside the whale's __(1)__ mouth. However, the whale's throat is very tiny. The whale could not __(2)__ a person.

_____ **1.** A. little   B. tremendous   C. hungry   D. tight

_____ **2.** A. taste   B. capture   C. swallow   D. find

The game of tennis began around eight hundred years ago. Players in France hit a ball over a net. However, they did not use a __(3)__ to play the game. They used the __(4)__ of their hands.

_____ **3.** A. mask   B. motor   C. trap   D. racket

_____ **4.** A. palms   B. nets   C. riddles   D. families

Your fingerprints are unlike those of any other person. Even twins have fingerprints that __(5)__ . Experts say that fingerprints are the best way to __(6)__ someone. These prints can help solve crimes.

_____ **5.** A. whisk   B. vary   C. flicker   D. advance

_____ **6.** A. huddle   B. invite   C. grasp   D. identify

Scientists say that black holes __(7)__ in space, although they cannot be seen. It is thought that black holes __(8)__ when huge stars cave in. If the sun became a black hole, it would be only four miles across.

_____ **7.** A. budge   B. gust   C. exist   D. lend

_____ **8.** A. leak   B. satisfy   C. admire   D. develop

Go on to the next page.

Name _____   Date _____

Read the story. Choose the answer that best completes the sentence.

The honeysucker, or honey possum, eats the **nectar** found in large flowers. To do this it sticks its long, thin nose into a flower. Then it uses its long, rough tongue to get the sticky food.

_____ **9.** In this paragraph the word **nectar** means
      A. fruit   C. sweet liquid
      B. roots   D. green leaves

In times long ago, a feast was more than just fancy food on a table. People dressed in fine clothing. Guests were often **entertained** with music, dancing, and juggling.

_____ **10.** In this paragraph the word **entertained** means
      A. starved   C. invited
      B. seated   D. amused

People have always feared the blasts of hot lava and ashes from a volcano. The power of a volcano has caused many disasters. In 1991 the explosion of a volcano in the Philippine Islands **demolished** an air force base. The base was completely covered with hot ash.

_____ **11.** In this paragraph the word **demolished** means
      A. built   C. destroyed
      B. visited   D. landed

A boomerang is made so that it returns to the person who throws it. A boomerang has two arms and a **curve** in the middle. This shape makes the boomerang spin. This spinning causes the boomerang to circle back to the person who threw it.

_____ **12.** In this paragraph the word **curve** means
      A. leg   C. belt
      B. well   D. bend

Name _____   Date _____

Read the story. Choose the answer that best completes each sentence.

Florida is on the southeastern coast of the United States. It has water on three sides. Since the __(1)__ is warm, there are many palm trees. There are also many beautiful beaches. For these reasons, many people __(2)__ in Florida.

_____ **1. A.** climate   **B.** size   **C.** rowboat   **D.** insect

_____ **2. A.** water   **B.** test   **C.** vacation   **D.** list

The first motion pictures were made in 1887. To see these movies, people looked through a hole in a box. Movies were later shown on a __(3)__ . Recordings were used for sound. Later, sound was put __(4)__ on the movie film.

_____ **3. A.** screen   **B.** oven   **C.** hive   **D.** tub

_____ **4. A.** sadly   **B.** happily   **C.** directly   **D.** angrily

Artists often use colors to __(5)__ feelings. Bright colors show happy feelings. Dark colors show sad feelings. When you look at a painting, you can tell what the artist's __(6)__ was.

_____ **5. A.** buy   **B.** eat   **C.** shovel   **D.** express

_____ **6. A.** height   **B.** mood   **C.** brush   **D.** meal

Nothing lives or grows on the moon. But scientists have discovered that some plants on Earth grow better if they are __(7)__ by the moon. If moon dust is __(8)__ over the plants, they grow much bigger. No one yet knows why.

_____ **7. A.** melted   **B.** aided   **C.** wet   **D.** arranged

_____ **8. A.** trusted   **B.** curved   **C.** sprinkled   **D.** chosen

Name _____   Date _____

Read the story. Choose the answer that best completes each sentence.

Our lives are filled with printed words. Books, newspapers, and
 _(1)_ use print. We buy _(2)_ that have information printed on them. Paper
money is printed. TV uses print. Even games use printed words.

_____ **1. A.** shoes   **B.** pictures   **C.** magazines   **D.** faces

_____ **2. A.** songs   **B.** stars   **C.** products   **D.** noise

Fishing is one of the most popular sports. You need special fishing _(3)_ if you want to
fish seriously. Most experts use a rod that is strong but _(4)_ so it won't break.

_____ **3. A.** types   **B.** tackle   **C.** news   **D.** bowls

_____ **4. A.** weak   **B.** famous   **C.** open   **D.** flexible

Certain walking races are called the "heel and toe." People walking in such races use a
special _(5)_ . They take very long _(6)_ . A heel-and-toe expert can walk one mile in six
and one-half minutes.

_____ **5. A.** technique   **B.** sink   **C.** fort   **D.** table

_____ **6. A.** strides   **B.** lines   **C.** pencils   **D.** sounds

Washington, D.C., was planned by George Washington. It became the _(7)_ of the
United States in 1800. Today many people live in the city. But many more people live in
the _(8)_ and travel to the city each day to work.

_____ **7. A.** library   **B.** chair   **C.** war   **D.** capital

_____ **8. A.** cars   **B.** suburbs   **C.** machines   **D.** farms

Name _____   Date _____

Read the story. Choose the answer that best completes each sentence.

The Statue of Liberty was __(1)__ in 210 separate pieces. The pieces were packed in __(2)__ . Then they were shipped from France to America. There the pieces were joined to form Miss Liberty.

_____ **1.** A. whole   B. originally   C. never   D. bent

_____ **2.** A. beds   B. nickels   C. lights   D. crates

The first kites were made about 2,500 years ago in China. They were made of large leaves. String had not been __(3)__ yet. The kite strings were made of twisted __(4)__ .

_____ **3.** A. shown   B. liked   C. wanted   D. invented

_____ **4.** A. vines   B. trees   C. tops   D. rows

Some people are __(5)__ that mice scare elephants. But these big beasts do not __(6)__ fear when they see a mouse. However, elephants will run away from a rabbit or a dog.

_____ **5.** A. clear   B. comfortable   C. hopeful   D. convinced

_____ **6.** A. enjoy   B. choose   C. exhibit   D. challenge

Columbus found many __(7)__ things to eat in the New World. When he went back to Europe, he carried some of these new foods with him. He gave the king and queen of Spain a __(8)__ . He offered them corn, peppers, pineapples, pumpkins, and sweet potatoes.

_____ **7.** A. hidden   B. secret   C. short   D. delicious

_____ **8.** A. banquet   B. carpet   C. princess   D. batter

Comprehension 6, SV 6188-5

Name _____   Date _____

Read the story. Choose the answer that best completes each sentence.

The first Olympic games were held in Greece. Boys between the ages of 12 and 17 entered the junior __(1)__ . At the age of 18, they could enter the __(2)__ contests.

_____ **1.** **A.** schools   **B.** darkness   **C.** events   **D.** grounds

_____ **2.** **A.** small   **B.** championship   **C.** fast   **D.** strange

Some bats have only one baby at a time. When the mother bat flies out at night, she carries her __(3)__ along with her. The young one hangs onto the mother as she __(4)__ through the dark.

_____ **3.** **A.** amount   **B.** sister   **C.** newborn   **D.** enemy

_____ **4.** **A.** swoops   **B.** blinks   **C.** motions   **D.** hatches

Plants need light in order to grow. But many plants __(5)__ to grow fast in the dark. Corn is one __(6)__ . It grows most quickly during warm summer nights.

_____ **5.** **A.** continue   **B.** burn   **C.** complete   **D.** dip

_____ **6.** **A.** flower   **B.** field   **C.** example   **D.** weed

On the __(7)__ person's head, there are about one hundred thousand hairs. When people are young, their hair grows fast. It grows about one hundredth of an inch a day. This __(8)__ growth slows down as people get older. If you never cut your hair in your life, it might grow to be 25 feet long.

_____ **7.** **A.** neat   **B.** old   **C.** average   **D.** noisy

_____ **8.** **A.** hard   **B.** rapid   **C.** sleepy   **D.** straight

Name _____   Date _____

Read the story. Choose the answer that best completes each sentence.

Dragons still live. The Komodo dragon in Asia is the largest living __(1)__ . It grows to be over ten feet long. It has a long tail, __(2)__ skin, and a wide red mouth.

_____ **1.** **A.** western   **B.** visitor   **C.** puppet   **D.** lizard

_____ **2.** **A.** thirsty   **B.** sweet   **C.** rough   **D.** private

Exercise can help people live longer. __(3)__ say that people who walk or run about half an hour each day stay in better __(4)__ . Some people say they don't have time to work out. They should take the time. For each hour a person exercises, that person may live an hour longer.

_____ **3.** **A.** Owners   **B.** Elephants   **C.** Experts   **D.** Uncles

_____ **4.** **A.** sunshine   **B.** order   **C.** matter   **D.** health

A woman said to a friend, "Yesterday I fell over forty feet." The friend __(5)__ , "That's just __(6)__ ! Were you hurt?" The first woman said, "No, I was just finding my seat at the movies."

_____ **5.** **A.** felt   **B.** exclaimed   **C.** discovered   **D.** bounced

_____ **6.** **A.** horrible   **B.** favor   **C.** silent   **D.** aboard

Some gardeners like to __(7)__ huge vegetables. A man in New England raised two giant __(8)__ for Halloween. Each one weighed 580 pounds!

_____ **7.** **A.** cultivate   **B.** pet   **C.** rake   **D.** believe

_____ **8.** **A.** ghosts   **B.** feasts   **C.** pumpkins   **D.** cats

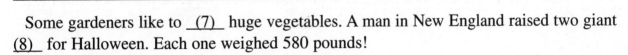

Comprehension 6, SV 6188-5

Name _____   Date _____

Read the story. Choose the answer that best completes each sentence.

In football the judge of every play is the __(1)__ . It is this person's job to decide when a __(2)__ must be given to a player or team that does something wrong.

_____ **1.** A. safety   B. referee   C. coach   D. yard

_____ **2.** A. penalty   B. reward   C. penny   D. season

People who fish dream about catching a ten-pound __(3)__ . These fish do not usually get that large. The ones that do are old and smart. It takes much __(4)__ , cleverness, and luck to outsmart such wise old fish.

_____ **3.** A. boat   B. worm   C. boot   D. bass

_____ **4.** A. rushing   B. snow   C. patience   D. pay

The New England Aquarium is in Massachusetts. Visitors have the __(5)__ to see how animals live in the water. Some animals thrill __(6)__ by performing in water shows.

_____ **5.** A. power   B. opportunity   C. itch   D. desert

_____ **6.** A. pipes   B. jewels   C. audiences   D. holidays

The cockatiel is a bird that looks like a parrot. But it has a __(7)__ of feathers on its head. The cockatiel makes a nice pet because it is __(8)__ and likes to be around people.

_____ **7.** A. crest   B. cup   C. tail   D. broom

_____ **8.** A. mean   B. messy   C. affectionate   D. scary

Name _____   Date _____

Read the story. Choose the answer that best completes the sentence.

Rosa Lee Parks is a **notable** figure in the civil rights movement. She refused to obey the law that said that black people must sit in the back of the bus. She won a medal for her courage.

_____ **1.** In this paragraph the word **notable** means
    A. sad   **C.** comfortable
    B. important   **D.** running

The first telephone in the White House was **installed** in 1877. Rutherford B. Hayes was president then. He ordered the new phone.

_____ **2.** In this paragraph the word **installed** means
    A. called up   **C.** removed
    B. fixed up   **D.** put in

Some people say the wolverine is the most **crafty** animal in the United States. It finds traps in the snow, then it follows the trail to the trapper's cabin. There the animal eats all the food and takes away the pots and pans.

_____ **3.** In this paragraph the word **crafty** means
    A. poor   **C.** clever
    B. mean   **D.** thirsty

Some plants develop seeds. These seeds develop into new plants. Seeds will not **sprout** until conditions are right. The seed must have the right temperature, water, and soil.

_____ **4.** In this paragraph the word **sprout** means
    A. break   **C.** begin to grow
    B. scratch   **D.** begin to die

Comprehension 6, SV 6188-5

Name _____   Date _____

Read the story. Choose the answer that best completes the sentence.

Many people wear black as a sign of **mourning**. In China the color for death is white. People in Turkey wear purple. But everywhere people follow special customs when someone dies.

_____ **1.** In this paragraph the word **mourning** means

    A. seeing dawn   **C.** showing joy

    B. feeling sick   **D.** showing sadness

The most common **source** of milk is the cow. The goat also gives milk. Other animals that give milk are the camel, buffalo, yak, reindeer, llama, and zebra.

_____ **2.** In this paragraph the word **source** means

    A. bottle   **C.** drink

    B. direction   **D.** supply

When Franz Liszt played the piano, he became **violent**. Often the keys would fly off the piano. Sometimes the strings of the piano would snap with the force of his blows.

_____ **3.** In this paragraph the word **violent** means

    A. rough   **C.** gentle

    B. purple   **D.** large

In 1608 Thomas Coryat brought a new custom to England. He had learned how to eat with a fork. At first the English didn't think this new way to eat was **appropriate**. They did not think it was a good idea. They did not begin to use forks until some time later.

_____ **4.** In this paragraph the word **appropriate** means

    A. fun   **C.** filling

    B. correct   **D.** magic

Comprehension 6, SV 6188-5

Name _____   Date _____

Read the story. Choose the answer that best completes the sentence.

When ducks **migrate** south each fall, many of them pass over Stuttgard, Arkansas. So the people there hold a duck-calling contest. As the ducks fly by, the people quack away!

_____ **1.** In this paragraph the word **migrate** means
     A. locate   **C.** travel
     B. mumble   **D.** honk

Have you ever seen a moonbow? It's like a rainbow, but it's made by the moon. Moonbows **occur** when the moon's light shines through the mist from a waterfall.

_____ **2.** In this paragraph the word **occur** means
     A. rain   **C.** happen
     B. flow   **D.** disappear

Once a man checked out a book from a library. He **neglected** to return it. The book was finally returned by his great-grandson 145 years later. Although the fine came to $2,264, the great-grandson did not have to pay it.

_____ **3.** In this paragraph the word **neglected** means
     A. hurried   **C.** borrowed
     B. failed   **D.** remembered

Every June **mobs** of people gather at Jensen Beach in Florida to watch for sea turtles. Hundreds of people snap pictures of the turtles as they lay their eggs.

_____ **4.** In this paragraph the word **mobs** means
     A. crowds   **C.** swimmers
     B. visitors   **D.** couples

Name _____   Date _____

Read the story. Choose the answer that best completes the sentence.

Clowns spend much time painting their faces. They don't want people to copy their design. Pictures of the clowns' faces are put in a file as a **permanent** record.

_____ **1.** In this paragraph the word **permanent** means
        A. playing   **C.** lasting
        B. pretty   **D.** broken

A **typical** American saying is *O.K.* There are many stories about how this saying got started. One story is that some writers in Boston were having fun. They used *O.K.* to stand for "oll korrect," a misspelling of "all correct."

_____ **2.** In this paragraph the word **typical** means
        A. usual   **C.** wild
        B. west   **D.** odd

Shirley Temple won an Oscar award for her **performance** in the movie *Bright Eyes*. She was in this movie when she was only six years old.

_____ **3.** In this paragraph the word **performance** means
        A. youth   **C.** acting
        B. sewing   **D.** dinner

The town of Young America, Minnesota, **sponsors** a bed-racing contest each year. People line up all sorts of beds on wheels. Then they roll them down the main street toward the finish line.

_____ **4.** In this paragraph the word **sponsors** means
        A. owns   **C.** sells
        B. wins   **D.** holds

Comprehension 6, SV 6188-5

Name _____   Date _____

Read the story. Choose the answer that best completes the sentence.

Long ago a bride's father gave all her shoes to her new husband. This **indicated** that the father no longer had to care for the bride. Today we keep this custom by tying shoes to a wedding car.

_____ **1.** In this paragraph the word **indicated** means
     A. behaved   **C.** prayed
     B. pained   **D.** meant

The oldest false teeth are almost three thousand years old. They were found on the body of a **deceased** person in an old grave. The teeth were strung together with gold wire.

_____ **2.** In this paragraph the word **deceased** means
     A. dead   **C.** healthy
     B. old   **D.** rich

Sir Robert Peel formed a special police force in London to fight crime. It was so **effective** that other towns started special forces, too. These police officers are now called bobbies, for Sir Robert's nickname.

_____ **3.** In this paragraph the word **effective** means
     A. ragged   **C.** quiet
     B. successful   **D.** proud

The bits of paper thrown during parades are called confetti. This word means "candy." Once people threw candy during **festive** and merry events. Now we throw paper.

_____ **4.** In this paragraph the word **festive** means
     A. worn   **C.** smooth
     B. tasty   **D.** jolly

Comprehension 6, SV 6188-5

Name _____   Date _____

Read the story. Choose the answer that best completes the sentence.

Do you like to hear the **booming** of thunder? Go to a place called Boga. People there hear thunder about 332 days of each year.

_____ 1. In this paragraph the word **booming** means
   A. raining   C. flashing
   B. tangle   D. crashing

The elephant has the largest ears in the animal kingdom. This **massive** beast needs them because its body is so big. An African elephant's ears can grow to be four feet across.

_____ 2. In this paragraph the word **massive** means
   A. tiny   C. huge
   B. chosen   D. fancy

The Purple Heart is an award given to members of the United States armed forces. It is given to those hurt or killed in **combat**.

_____ 3. In this paragraph the word **combat** means
   A. traffic   C. parades
   B. fighting   D. hunting

It is thought that Hanson Crockett Gregory invented the doughnut hole. Long ago, doughnuts had no holes. Gregory thought those doughnuts were soggy in the middle. So he **recommended** that his mother make a hole in one. It cooked better that way.

_____ 4. In this paragraph the word **recommended** means
   A. suggested   C. refused
   B. forgot   D. doubted

Name _____   Date _____

Read the story. Choose the answer that best completes the sentence.

1. Every year in Hollywood there is a contest for people who perform stunts. The contest has three main events. In the horse event, the stunt people must make their horses fall. Then they jump on other horses and race down a long trail. In the motorcycle event, people race eight laps around a dirt track. In the last event, they race around the dirt track in cars.

_____   The story mainly tells

     A. how Hollywood gets money

     B. how motorcycles are raced

     C. what a stunt contest is like

     D. when dirt track racing began

2. Playing football was once against the law. In England years ago, King Henry II thought that his soldiers weren't practicing with their bows and arrows. He blamed football and declared that people who played the game would be thrown in prison. For years nobody played. Later, soldiers used guns instead of bows and arrows. The new king decided to let soldiers play football once again.

_____   The story mainly tells

     A. how English people liked football

     B. when football was against the law

     C. when King Henry II made announcements

     D. how bows and arrows were used in war

3. You dream each night, even though you may not remember your dreams. While you dream your eyes move and your heart beats faster. Even your brain-wave pattern changes. Some scientists think that dreaming is important for the sake of health. They claim that without dreams, people would go crazy.

_____   The story mainly tells

     A. how people stay healthy

     B. how sleep is necessary

     C. why dreams are important

     D. when people remember their dreams

Go on to the next page.

Name _____   Date _____

4. A baby sleeps about 18 hours a day. A child who is 10 years old sleeps about 10 hours. Adults need between 7 and 8 hours of sleep each day. Older people can get by on little sleep. They need only about 6 hours every night.

_____   The story mainly tells

      A. how people go crazy without sleep

      B. how babies sleep

      C. how much sleep people need

      D. how many hours teenagers sleep

5. In America we have Halloween. In Mexico they have *Todos Santos,* which means "All Saints." This is the day in which people remember family and friends who have died. They visit the cemetery instead of going out to trick-or-treat. But they do have pictures of skeletons and ghosts hanging around. They also have many candy skulls to eat.

_____   The story mainly tells

      A. what holidays are like

      B. what Halloween is like in Mexico

      C. what happens during *Todos Santos*

      D. what we do on Halloween

6. A few years ago, a man in Los Angeles got a special license plate for his car. It read *NONE.* After two weeks he got a bill for parking tickets. The total was almost one thousand dollars! He was sure that it was a mistake. He found out the reason for his huge bill. If a car doesn't have a license plate, the police just write *none* in the blank on the parking ticket. The man got new plates right away!

_____   The story mainly tells

      A. what to do when you get a lot of parking tickets

      B. about a problem with special license plates

      C. what the police wrote on the ticket

      D. how to avoid getting tickets

Name _____   Date _____

Read the story. Choose the answer that best completes the sentence.

1. Today there are gyms for people who use wheelchairs. These people can lift weights or get a tan. Teams of people can get together for a game of basketball. Being in a wheelchair doesn't have to mean just sitting around!

_____   The story mainly tells

     A. how some people use wheelchairs
     B. where people in wheelchairs can exercise
     C. how to work out for good health
     D. how to lift weights on special machines

2. The sport of logrolling was invented by lumberjacks. *Lumberjacks* are workers who cut down trees and float the logs down the river to the lumber mills. For fun, these people hold contests. Two lumberjacks stand on a log in the river and try to make each other fall off by rolling the log with their feet.

_____   The story mainly tells

     A. about the sport of logrolling
     B. where lumberjacks work
     C. how to float logs
     D. where to saw lumber

3. Cats are very hard to train, but some people have figured out how to do it. The secret is that a cat's brain is in its stomach. All you need is cat food, a spoon, and plenty of time! Put some food on the spoon and hold it wherever you want the cat to go. The cat will learn to obey your hand motions, even when there isn't any food.

_____   The story mainly tells

     A. how to teach an old dog new tricks
     B. where the parts of a cat are located
     C. how to train a cat
     D. the differences between cats and dogs

Name _____   Date _____

Read the story. Choose the answer that best completes the sentence.

1. *Equinox* means "equal night." Two times during the year, day and night last exactly 12 hours each. The vernal, or spring, equinox takes place about March 21. It marks the beginning of spring. The autumnal equinox is on September 22 or 23. It marks the start of autumn.

March

Sun	Mon	Tues	Wed	Thur	Fri	Sat
			1	2	3	4
5	6	7	8	9	10	11
12	13	14	15	16	17	18
19	20	21	22	23	24	25
26	27	28	29	30	31	

_____   The story mainly tells

   A. about the two equinoxes
   B. when summer begins
   C. about the way in which an equinox lasts 28 hours
   D. that each season begins with an equinox

2. The steeplechase is a difficult horse race. The riders race over many ditches and barriers. It began in Ireland in 1803. A group of fox hunters decided to race toward a distant church steeple over a straight course. During the race the riders had to jump over anything that stood in their way. Because the steeple was the goal of such a race, it became known as the steeplechase.

_____   The story mainly tells

   A. about the kind of horses used in a steeplechase
   B. how steeplechasing happens only in Ireland
   C. about the different kinds of horse races
   D. about the race known as the steeplechase

3. James Weldon Johnson wrote a poem about freedom. In 1900 his brother John set the poem to music. The name of the song was "Lift Every Voice and Sing." It was called the Negro National Anthem. The song begins with "Lift every voice and sing, 'til earth and heaven ring. Ring with the harmonies of liberty." Today African Americans still sing this song with pride.

_____   The story mainly tells

   A. that James Weldon Johnson wrote many poems
   B. that John Johnson wrote many poems
   C. that "Lift Every Voice and Sing" was never sung
   D. about a song still sung by African Americans

Name _____   Date _____

Read the story. Choose the answer that best completes the sentence.

---

1. Birds have big appetites. Many birds eat as much as half their weight in worms and insects every day. The American robin eats about 70 worms in a day. Baby birds digest their food very quickly. Some birds feed their hungry babies as many as 20 times an hour. Baby titmice are fed as many as 480 times in a day!

_____   The story mainly tells

      A. about the foods that birds eat
      B. how baby titmice eat
      C. how much birds eat every day
      D. that birds have small appetites

---

2. The first nonstop flight across the Atlantic Ocean was made in June 1919. Two British men, John Alcock and Arthur Brown, flew sixteen and one-half hours across the ocean. At one time during the trip, Brown had to crawl out onto the wings to remove the ice.

_____   The story mainly tells

      A. how many times Alcock and Brown flew
      B. that Alcock and Brown had never flown before
      C. about the first nonstop flight across the Pacific
      D. about the first nonstop flight across the Atlantic

---

3. Have you ever hit your elbow and felt a shooting pain in your arm and hand? People call this area the funny bone. But did you know that the funny bone is not a bone at all? It's really a nerve that runs under the upper part of the arm, stretching from the shoulder to the elbow. The long bone there is called the humerus. Because of the name of this bone, this nerve got its *humorous* name.

_____   The story mainly tells that

      A. the funny bone is a bone found in the elbow
      B. the funny bone is a nerve
      C. it tickles when the funny bone is hit
      D. the funny bone is in the lower part of the arm

Name _____   Date _____

Read the story. Choose the answer that best completes the sentence.

1. A human baby is born without teeth. As an adult he or she will have 32 permanent teeth. A baby grows a set of 20 baby teeth before a set of permanent teeth. One by one, the baby teeth fall out as the permanent teeth begin to appear. By the age of 25, a person has a full set of 32 permanent teeth.

_____   The story mainly tells

    A. about baby and permanent teeth

    B. what teeth are made of

    C. at what age baby teeth are lost

    D. how long it takes teeth to grow

2. Bees and wasps are alike in many ways. But there are big differences between the two insects. Wasps are slimmer, more brightly colored, and less hairy than bees. While a worker bee can sting only once, a wasp can sting several times. Bees make their nests from wax, while wasps make them out of paper and mud. Bees, not wasps, make honey to feed their young. While many wasps are meat-eating, bees are not. They don't eat spiders, flies, or caterpillars.

_____   The story mainly tells

    A. about the ways that bees and wasps are alike

    B. how bees and wasps are different

    C. how bees build their nests

    D. why wasps and bees sting

3. The year 1972 was important for Yvonne Burke. It was the year in which she turned forty, got married, and ran for the United States Congress. She was selected Woman of the Year by the *Los Angeles Times* and the National Association of Black Manufacturers. She was also named as one of America's two hundred future leaders by *Time* magazine.

_____   The story mainly tells that

    A. 1972 was a difficult year for Burke

    B. Burke won election to the Senate

    C. 1972 was a successful year for Burke

    D. Burke was *Time* magazine's Woman of the Year

Name _____   Date _____

Read the story. Choose the answer that best completes the sentence.

1. Did you know that when a sheep falls down, it cannot get up again by itself? A sheep has a heavy body but delicate legs. When it's lying on its back, it's weighted down by its thick, heavy fleece. Even waving its legs doesn't help. Its legs are too thin and weak to swing its heavy body onto its side. A shepherd has to help the sheep back onto its feet!

_____ The story mainly tells

    A. how a sheep uses its legs to get up

    B. that a sheep never falls down

    C. why a sheep can't get itself up when it falls down

    D. how a sheep uses its fleece to get up

2. Are you one of those people who is bothered more than others by mosquitoes? If you are, there are ways to help prevent mosquitoes from biting. Dark colors and rough textures attract mosquitoes. If you will be outdoors, wear pale, smooth clothing instead of jeans. Some scents attract mosquitoes. So don't wear perfume or after-shave lotion, and be careful about the shampoo you use. Even scented shampoo can attract a bite!

_____ The story mainly tells

    A. why mosquitoes bite

    B. why mosquito bites itch

    C. how to prevent mosquitoes from biting

    D. how mosquitoes are attracted to yellow clothing

3. There is an easy way to find out how far away a thunderstorm is from you. Count the number of seconds between the flash of lightning and the clap of thunder. Then divide this number by five. This will tell you about how many miles away the lightning has struck. If you see the flash and hear the thunder at the same time, the storm is directly overhead.

_____ The story mainly tells

    A. how to find out how far away a thunderstorm is

    B. where lightning and thunder come from

    C. how to guess when a thunderstorm will end

    D. how to figure out the direction of a storm

         Comprehension 6, SV 6188-5

Name _____   Date _____

Read the story. Choose the answer that best completes the sentence.

_____

1. Frederic Bartholdi was the French sculptor of the Statue of Liberty. When Bartholdi was a student in France, there was a wall built to keep out the enemy. One night a girl carrying a torch jumped over the wall and yelled, "Forward!" The enemy soldiers shot her. Years later Bartholdi remembered the girl with the torch in her hand. It gave him an idea. Bartholdi used his wife as the model for the shape of the statue. His mother served as the model for the statue's face.

_____   The story mainly tells

      A. how Bartholdi got the idea for the Statue of Liberty

      B. how Bartholdi used himself as a model

      C. how a young girl designed the Statue of Liberty

      D. how soldiers shot at the Statue of Liberty

_____

2. When Millard Fillmore was 19, he could hardly read or write. He lived on a farm. He spent more time working than going to school. But later he decided to return to school. Abigail Powers was Fillmore's teacher. They fell in love, and later they were married. Fillmore went on to become a teacher, a lawyer, and the President of the United States!

_____   The story mainly tells that

      A. Fillmore never learned to read and write

      B. Fillmore went to school as an adult

      C. Fillmore taught Abigail Powers to read

      D. Fillmore never married

_____

3. In 1849 a mapmaker in Alaska was working on a map of the coastline. None of his maps showed a name for one of the capes. A *cape* is a point of land that juts out into the sea. So he wrote *Name?* on the map and sent it to his mapmaking company in England. A worker at the map company thought the man had written *Nome* on the map. Since then the city has been known as Nome, Alaska.

_____   The story mainly tells

      A. how maps are made

      B. how Nome, Alaska, got its name

      C. how the mapmaker traveled around Alaska

      D. how Alaska got its name

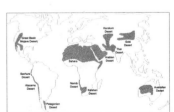

_____

Name _____   Date _____

Read the story. Choose the answer that best completes the sentence.

---

1. Mark Twain wrote a book titled *The Adventures of Tom Sawyer.* In this book, he told about some things he did as a child in the town of Hannibal, Missouri. Each year on the Fourth of July, this town has a special event called Tom Sawyer Days. People come from all over to celebrate. There is a parade, a raft race, a fence-painting contest, and a frog race. There is a big fireworks show held on the last night. It's just the kind of thing Tom Sawyer would have loved.

_____   The story mainly tells
- **A.** what Mark Twain's book is about
- **B.** what Tom Sawyer Days are like
- **C.** where to see a frog race
- **D.** where Mark Twain grew up

---

2. The heads of four men are carved into Mount Rushmore. They are Presidents Washington, Jefferson, Lincoln, and Roosevelt. Most of the work was done with dynamite. Workers carved the details with air hammers. They worked from cages and swings that hung from the top of the mountain. It took six and one-half years to finish the job.

_____   The story mainly tells
- **A.** how the carvings were made
- **B.** which Presidents are carved on the mountain
- **C.** how to work on top of Mount Rushmore
- **D.** how mountain carvers do their jobs

---

3. Some of the first cars were built with steam engines. In those days most cars that used gas could travel only about twenty miles an hour. However, one car that used steam traveled more than one hundred miles an hour. People stopped using steam engines when large amounts of oil were discovered. Today oil is growing scarce. People are trying to find out if we could use steam or electricity instead of gas to run cars in the future.

_____   The story mainly tells
- **A.** how coal replaced the steam in engines
- **B.** why cars were built to run with steam engines
- **C.** when large amounts of oil were discovered
- **D.** which fuels have powered cars

Name _____ Date _____

Read the story. Choose the answer that best completes the sentence.

---

1. Doctors have studied the ways in which children get hurt in the face. The doctors asked, "Which is worse, car accidents or sports accidents?" The doctors found that falling off bicycles causes the most injuries to the face. In one year, seventy thousand children hurt their faces in bicycle accidents. They had everything from broken noses to missing teeth.

_____ The story mainly tells

    A. the most common way children hurt their faces

    B. how to ride a bicycle

    C. how many children had accidents

    D. where the children were injured

---

2. Babies like things that are sweet, but they aren't fond of most other flavors. As children grow up, they start liking sour and bitter flavors. Experts think that flavors start tasting different to children between the ages of 12 and 14. At one time people studied children and coffee. Those younger than 14 didn't like the taste of coffee. But children older than 14 did like it.

_____ The story mainly tells

    A. how people's sense of taste changes

    B. how much children like coffee

    C. what happens when children are 14 years old

    D. which foods babies like

---

3. Long ago many people in Egypt worshipped a goddess that had a cat's head. She was the goddess of the sun and moon. People prayed to her for rain and good crops. Because cats were a symbol of the goddess, killing a cat was a serious crime. When a cat died, its owners shaved off their eyebrows as a sign of mourning.

_____ The story mainly tells

    A. how a cat became a goddess

    B. how ancient Egyptians felt about cats

    C. why killing a cat was a serious crime

    D. how cats were buried after they died

Name _____   Date _____

Read the story. Choose the answer that best completes the sentence.

_____

1. Do you ever wonder how games are invented? James Naismith was teaching a class when he made up a new game. He combined the games of lacrosse and soccer. But the players neither used a stick as in lacrosse nor did they kick a ball as in soccer. Instead they bounced, or dribbled, the ball and shot at a goal. The only thing Naismith had to use as a goal was a peach basket. This is why he decided to call the game basketball.

_____   The story mainly tells

    A. how to play lacrosse

    B. how Naismith taught physical education classes

    C. how the game of basketball was invented

    D. that a ball is kicked in soccer

2. Winston Churchill, the Prime Minister of Great Britain, is remembered for his great speeches. But as a boy, Churchill had trouble speaking. He stuttered. As a teenager he found a way to control his stuttering. He began each sentence by saying "mmmmm." Although this took care of his problem, he continued to do this for the rest of his life.

_____   The story mainly tells that

    A. Churchill had a speech problem

    B. Churchill would not speak in public

    C. Churchill stuttered because he had no tongue

    D. Churchill started stuttering as a teenager

3. In the South during the 1950s, it was against the law for whites and African Americans to attend the same college. James Meredith challenged this injustice. Constance Motley was the lawyer who defended James Meredith's rights in court. She won his case against the University of Mississippi. Constance Motley continued the fight for civil rights.

_____   The story mainly tells that

    A. Motley helped fight for civil rights

    B. Meredith helped Motley go to college

    C. Motley went to the University of Mississippi

    D. Motley did not believe in civil rights

Name _____   Date _____

Read the story. Choose the answer that best completes the sentence.

1. Is it possible to eat healthy food at a fast-food restaurant? You could drink orange juice or low-fat milk instead of a malt or a milk shake. You could try a whole-grain bun rather than the regular white one on your sandwich. A baked potato instead of fried potatoes would be a healthy choice. But you'll need to have the potato plain rather than with all the trimmings!

_____ The story mainly tells

    A. about the most popular fast foods
    B. healthy ways to eat at fast-food restaurants
    C. that all fast food is junk food
    D. how fried potatoes are a healthy choice

2. In 1905 the Colorado River flooded parts of Nevada. It ruined crops, roads, and buildings. Water covered the land for an entire year. To stop the flooding, the construction of Hoover Dam began. The dam controlled the river and brought water to the cities. It was completed in 1935. It took 5,000 workers and 5 years to build. Hoover Dam is 1,244 feet long and 726 feet high.

_____ The story mainly tells

    A. why Hoover Dam was built
    B. how the Colorado River runs through Nevada
    C. how Hoover Dam caused flooding in Nevada
    D. how Hoover Dam is the largest dam in the world

3. The space program wanted to send a teacher into space along with the six astronauts. Thousands of people applied to become the first teacher in space. A high-school teacher from New Hampshire was selected. Her name was Christa McAuliffe. When asked about the historic mission, McAuliffe replied, "I want to give an ordinary person's view of space." In 1986 the spacecraft, *Challenger,* exploded shortly after takeoff. Everyone aboard was killed.

_____ The story mainly tells

    A. why the *Challenger* exploded
    B. how McAuliffe was trained as an astronaut
    C. that McAuliffe was chosen for the space flight
    D. that McAuliffe joined the five-member crew

Name _____   Date _____

Read the story. Choose the answer that best completes the sentence.

1. In 1898 Morgan Robertson wrote a book. His book was about a ship, the *Titan*, that carried many rich, powerful people. On an April night, the ship hit an iceberg in the North Atlantic Ocean. It sunk. The ship did not have enough lifeboats for all its passengers. Many people died. Fourteen years later there was a real ship, the *Titanic*. It hit an iceberg at night in the North Atlantic in April 1912. Just like the *Titan*, it didn't have enough lifeboats for everyone. Many passengers died. Unfortunately, many parts of Robertson's story came true.

_____   The story mainly tells that
- A. Robertson was a passenger on the *Titanic*
- B. the *Titan* was a real ship
- C. the passengers on the *Titan* were poor people
- D. a story about a shipwreck came true

2. Which kind of clam chowder do you prefer? In the United States, there are two kinds of clam chowder. *Manhattan* clam chowder is made with tomatoes. *New England* clam chowder is made with milk. People from Massachusetts take their clam chowder very seriously. In fact, they passed a law that does not allow clam chowder with tomatoes in their state!

_____   The story mainly tells
- A. the difference between two clam chowders
- B. about the many different kinds of clam chowder
- C. that clam chowder is a kind of soup
- D. that there is only one way to make clam chowder

3. Puerto Rico gave women the right to vote in 1932. Felisa de Rincón Gautier was asked to be the mayor of San Juan. Her reply was that a "woman mayor" was not the custom. But two years later, Gautier changed her mind. She became the first woman mayor of Puerto Rico. She was the mayor of San Juan for 22 years.

_____   The story mainly tells that
- A. women cannot vote in Puerto Rico today
- B. San Juan would not elect a woman mayor
- C. Gautier proved that women can be mayors
- D. Gautier lost the election for mayor of San Juan

Name _____   Date _____

Read the story. Choose the answer that best completes the sentence.

---

1. During the 1850s Levi Strauss moved to San Francisco. He sold canvas material used for making tents and covered wagons. Gold miners and railroad workers complained that their pants tore easily or became worn too soon. So Strauss used his canvas to make a pair of pants. He called the pants after himself, or Levi's. They sold for twenty-two cents a pair. Later Strauss made a pair of denim pants and dyed them blue.

_____ The story mainly tells

    A. why Levi Strauss moved to San Francisco

    B. that Levi Strauss was a gold miner

    C. that the first Levi's were brown

    D. that Levi Strauss invented the first blue jeans

---

2. Movie stars were the first people to wear sunglasses. Early movie lights were very bright and hurt the eyes. Actors wore sunglasses to rest their eyes. Today sunglasses are very popular. People wear them to protect their eyes from the sun.

_____ The story mainly tells

    A. how sunglasses were made

    B. who invented sunglasses

    C. why movie stars wore sunglasses

    D. that movie stars wanted to look mysterious

---

3. Isabella Baumfree was born a slave. When New York outlawed slavery, her master would not set her free. So Baumfree escaped. She changed her name to Sojourner Truth. She chose the name because she hoped to speak out against slavery. Truth traveled all over the North, spreading her message against slavery. As a result she was beaten many times. But that didn't stop her. Luckily, Truth lived to see the day in which slavery was outlawed throughout the country.

_____ The story mainly tells

    A. that Truth lived in New York

    B. that Truth fought to end slavery everywhere

    C. the year in which slavery was outlawed

    D. that Isabella Baumfree was a slave all her life

Name _____   Date _____

Read the story. Choose the answer that best completes the sentence.

---

1. One night during World War II, a duck in a city park in Freiburg, Germany, began squawking and flapping its wings. The duck had done this once before when bombs were dropped. This time, people heard the duck and ran for cover. Soon the bombing began. Today there is a statue of the duck in the park. It died in the attack.

_____   This story has a sad twist because

        A. people didn't pay attention to the duck's warnings

        B. the bombing began just before the duck made noise

        C. the duck was killed in the attack

        D. the statue doesn't look anything like the duck

---

2. Do you ever awaken right before the alarm clock rings? Experts know that people have "clocks" inside their bodies. The clock divides time into about 24 hours. Jet lag, or feeling tired and grumpy after traveling by plane, is a result of upsetting that inner clock.

_____   From this story you can tell that jet lag

        A. happens when a person's inner clock is off schedule

        B. has nothing to do with the body's inner clock

        C. goes away after your watch is reset

        D. is something from which experts seldom suffer

---

3. The Baseball Hall of Fame is in Cooperstown, New York. This site was chosen because it is where Abner Doubleday said that he invented the game in 1839. But baseball began in England. It started from a game called rounders. The word *baseball* is mentioned in English books as early as 1798.

_____   This story suggests that Abner Doubleday

        A. began the game of *rounders*

        B. coined the word *baseball* but not the game

        C. invented the game but not the word *baseball*

        D. received credit for something he didn't really do

Go on to the next page.

67

Name _____   Date _____

4. Jim clutched the wheel so tightly that his knuckles stuck out against his skin. The woman next to him turned the key. She said, "Now just start out slowly down the street. To change direction you need to turn the wheel only slightly." Jim pressed his foot down carefully.

_____   You can tell from this story that Jim
- **A.** is teaching the woman to drive
- **B.** is relaxed and confident
- **C.** is taking driving lessons from the woman
- **D.** is leaving the dock in a motorboat

5. Roberta put the key into the slot and turned it. She pulled out four envelopes that were inside the little box. She flipped through the first three quickly, muttering "bill" at each one. When she reached the fourth envelope, she stopped. Then she grinned and ripped the flap open.

_____   You can tell that Roberta probably received
- **A.** many letters from a friend named Bill
- **B.** three bills
- **C.** money in the fourth envelope
- **D.** quite a bit of mail every day

6. The first drop sent up a tiny cloud of dust and then disappeared. A rattlesnake slithered away from the unexpected sight. More drops followed, but they too were quickly lost in the dry sand. Then the drops increased. Puddles began to form among the cactus plants.

_____   The story is a description of
- **A.** rain falling in a desert after a dry period
- **B.** a sprinkler system in a zoo
- **C.** someone watering a lawn
- **D.** a storm beginning in the mountains

Comprehension 6, SV 6188-5

Name _____   Date _____

Read the story. Choose the answer that best completes the sentence.

1. Why do people sneeze? Scientists aren't sure why, but they know that sneezing can be a sign of illness. The Greeks at one time believed that one of their gods had invented sneezing. The early Romans believed that sneezing helped people make smart decisions. People in Europe thought that sneezing was a symbol of good health. So any patient who sneezed three times was always released from the hospital.

_____   From this story you can tell that
   A. sneezing has improved through the years
   B. the early Greeks were the first to sneeze
   C. ideas about sneezing have changed over time
   D. most people sneeze only three times

2. People in England used to hold many handwriting contests. The winner usually received a gold pen. In one contest the judges could not decide between two men who wrote beautifully. The judges looked at the handwriting samples for days. They found that one of the men had forgotten to dot an *i*. Because of this the other man walked away with the gold pen.

_____   One man lost the contest because he   *Trudy Kennedy*
   A. did not want the gold pen
   B. could not write beautifully
   C. forgot an important part of a letter
   D. did not follow the rules of the contest

3. When our country was new, most people lived on farms. About 95 out of every 100 people made their living by growing food. They ate the food they grew and sold whatever was left over to the people in cities. Today only about 2 out of every 100 people are farmers.

_____   Over time, Americans have been
   A. eating less and less
   B. moving away from farms
   C. moving out of towns and cities
   D. buying more farmland

Name _____   Date _____

Read the story. Choose the answer that best completes the sentence.

1. Alice Walker is a famous writer today. She was born in Georgia in 1944. As a child she was blind in one eye. This greatly affected her young life. Because she was African American, she was troubled by race problems, too. After college she joined the civil rights movement. She began writing and teaching. Today her stories deal mostly with the problems of women and racism.

_____   The story suggests that Alice Walker

    A. writes about her own problems in her stories

    B. was born in Oregon

    C. joined the civil rights movement in 1940

    D. became deaf as a child

2. The longest river in the world is the Nile. It runs through North Africa. The Nile is more than four thousand miles long. But the Nile is just one hundred miles longer than the Amazon River. The Amazon is found in South America.

_____   From the story you can tell that

    A. the Amazon is longer than the Nile

    B. the Nile is in South America

    C. the Nile and Amazon are very long rivers

    D. the Amazon is only one hundred miles long

3. Modern weddings are full of traditions. Some of these traditions date back to ancient times. Even today many brides wear veils when they marry. This comes from an ancient Spartan practice. At that time the bride used the veil to hide from evil spirits. Even the bridesmaids were meant to hide the bride away from evil spirits. The bride would surround herself with girls her own age in order to confuse the evil spirits. Only the groom could recognize her then.

_____   You can conclude that

    A. the groom is an evil spirit

    B. the Spartans were afraid of evil spirits

    C. evil spirits like wedding cakes

    D. bridesmaids help evil spirits find the bride

Name _____   Date _____

Read the story. Choose the answer that best completes the sentence.

---

1. Peter Salem was a soldier in the American Revolution. Salem was a slave, as were most African Americans at the time. But he was set free to join the army. He fought bravely at Concord and Lexington and was a hero at Bunker Hill. Salem took part in many more battles, too. After the war ended, the United States became a free nation. Salem became a free man.

_____   From the story you can tell that Peter Salem

    A. had to become a slave again after the war

    B. joined the British Army

    C. fought for himself and the freedom of his country

    D. was a coward

---

2. Most babies learn to talk by imitating the sounds they hear. Babies first babble, and later they are able to say words. A new study on babies has made some amazing discoveries. The study shows that deaf babies with deaf parents also babble, but they babble with their hands. They imitate the sign language that their parents use.

_____   The story suggests that

    A. all parents babble

    B. deaf babies learn to communicate by imitating

    C. all parents know sign language

    D. deaf babies babble with their toes

---

3. Fannie Lou Hamer grew up in the South. Like many other African Americans there, she was poor. Life was hard, and her people had few rights. In 1962 Fannie was fed up. She wanted to change things. She registered to vote but was arrested for no reason. Bullets were fired at her. She was even beaten. Still she worked to gain voting rights for all people. In 1965 her dream came true. Congress passed a voting-rights bill.

_____   The story suggests that Fannie Lou Hamer

    A. liked being poor

    B. was arrested for running a stop sign

    C. never achieved her goal

    D. had a dangerous fight to win her rights

Name _____ Date _____

Read the story. Choose the answer that best completes the sentence.

_____

1. When people marry they often exchange wedding rings. The rings are symbols of the love that the married couple share. But in many marriages, only the woman wears a ring. This practice goes back to ancient times. During that time many wives were captured or bought. These women wore rings to show that they were the property of their husbands.

_____ You can conclude that
- **A.** most wives are still purchased today
- **B.** the meaning of some wedding customs has changed
- **C.** wedding rings are worn in the nose
- **D.** couples should no longer marry

_____

2. Chiang Kai-shek was a famous Chinese leader. As a young man, he gained much power in China. He led the Chinese Army against the Japanese in World War II. After the war the Communists tried to take over China. Kai-shek fought bravely against them, but he lost the fight. With his followers he fled to Taiwan. Until his death he continued to fight against the Communist rule of China.

_____ The story suggests that Chiang Kai-shek
- **A.** believed that China should remain a free country
- **B.** is still the leader of China
- **C.** fled to Japan
- **D.** was a Communist

_____

3. Seashores experience a daily change in water level. This change is called tide. As the water is pulled from shore, the water level drops. This is known as low tide. As the water returns to shore, the water level rises. This is called high tide. The coming and going of the water is caused by the pull of the moon's gravity.

_____ You can tell from the story that
- **A.** tides are caused by the gravity of the sun
- **B.** the water level drops at high tide
- **C.** the moon has a strong effect on the earth's seas
- **D.** a *tide* is a change in water temperature

Name _____   Date _____

Read the story. Choose the answer that best completes the sentence.

1. Columns and columns of rock stand along the coast of Ireland. They make up a natural wonder called the Giant's Causeway. An old story says that this bridge was built by a character named Finn MacCool. He was building a bridge so that giants could walk from Ireland to Scotland.

_____ From this story you can tell that

    A. the causeway must be small

    B. the causeway must be new

    C. MacCool didn't really build the causeway

    D. giants still walk across the causeway

2. Our Constitution gives people freedom of speech. But that does not mean that people can say whatever they want. What if someone was in a store and wanted to cause trouble? The person could shout "Fire!" even if there wasn't any fire. Everyone would run out of the store at once, and people could get hurt. In this case the guilty person would not be protected under the freedom-of-speech laws.

_____ You can conclude that our laws

    A. are unfair to people

    B. cause trouble in stores

    C. may not protect people who lie

    D. let people say whatever they want

3. The porcupine uses the quills on its tail to defend itself. When an animal comes too close, the porcupine slaps its tail at the enemy. The sharp quills come off easily. They stick into the other creature's skin. Each quill has a hook at the end. This makes the quills very painful to remove.

_____ If the quills didn't have hooks, they would

    A. not stay on the porcupine

    B. come out more easily

    C. hurt much more

    D. shoot through the air

Name _____   Date _____

Read the story. Choose the answer that best completes the sentence.

1.   The first eyeglasses were probably made in China. With the printing of books in Europe in the 1400s, more people needed glasses. Ben Franklin invented bifocal glasses. The lenses on these glasses have two parts. One section is designed to correct for close vision, while the other section corrects for distant vision.

_____   You can conclude that before the 1400s

   A. most people wore glasses
   B. most people had good eyesight
   C. people didn't read much
   D. many people wore bifocals

2.   You've probably bought a soft drink from a vending machine. Did you ever wonder how the machine knows that you're using a real coin, such as a dime? When you put your dime in the slot, the machine weighs the coin. If its weight is correct, the machine then measures its size. Finally the machine makes sure that there are notches on the edge of the dime.

_____   You can conclude that vending machines

   A. aren't easy to fool
   B. don't take real dimes
   C. accept coins smaller than dimes
   D. accept wooden dimes

3.   Have you ever seen barnacles on a dock or a boat? When these shellfish are small, they have only 1 eye and 6 pairs of legs. As they get older, they have 2 more eyes, 12 pairs of legs, and 2 big feelers. In their final stage of growth, barnacles lose their eyes and attach themselves to another object for the rest of their lives.

_____   From this story you can tell that barnacles

   A. remain the same throughout their lives
   B. can see better when they are old
   C. pass through three stages of life
   D. are delicious to eat

Name _____   Date _____

Read the story. Choose the answer that best completes the sentence.

1. When Bessie Smith was a young girl, both of her parents died. But Smith's love of music helped her through hard times. By the age of nine, Smith was singing on street corners for spare change, and ten years later, Smith was singing the blues in cities throughout the South. Despite a life full of trouble and hardship, Smith managed to survive because of her music. Before her death in 1937, she was known throughout the world as the Empress of the Blues.

_____   From the story you can tell that Smith
    A. was rewarded for her love of music
    B. couldn't sing very well
    C. had a happy childhood
    D. is still alive today

2. Born in Costa Rica, Franklin Chang-Díaz dreamed all his young life of flying in space. At the age of 17, he moved to the United States. He couldn't speak English, but he learned it quickly and became a top student. Then in 1980 Franklin was selected as an astronaut. He trained hard to reach his goal. In 1986 his boyhood dream came true. He soared through space on the shuttle *Columbia*.

_____   From this story you <u>cannot</u> tell
    A. where Chang-Díaz was born
    B. about the boyhood dream of Chang-Díaz
    C. how many astronauts flew with Chang-Díaz
    D. when Chang-Díaz flew in space

3. Scientists know that cars and factories cause pollution. This pollution can make the earth's heat rise. But did you know that the belching of cows is also a problem? When cows belch, they produce the gas methane. Methane can worsen the greenhouse effect.

_____   From the story you <u>cannot</u> tell
    A. which things cause pollution
    B. what cow belching produces
    C. whether cow belching is a problem
    D. how many times a cow belches each day

Name _____   Date _____

Read the story. Choose the answer that best completes the sentence.

1. Do you like vanilla ice cream? This tasty treat gets its flavor from the vanilla bean. Many vanilla beans come from vines in Mexico. The beans are slender, yellow pods full of tiny, black seeds. In fact, *vanilla* means "little pod" in Spanish. The beans are picked and cured by heating. Then they are chopped and mixed with alcohol. The vanilla flavoring is then strained and bottled.

_____   From the story you <u>cannot</u> tell

     A. where vanilla beans come from
     B. how much flavoring is put in vanilla ice cream
     C. what *vanilla* means in Spanish
     D. how vanilla beans are cured

2. Mary Cassatt was a famous American painter. She was born in 1844. As a girl she traveled to Paris. There she gained a love of painting. As a young woman, she returned to Paris to study art. Her talent soon became well known. She painted mostly women and children in daily life. Around 1900 her eyesight began to fail. Her artwork suffered greatly. By World War I, her eyesight was so poor that she could no longer paint at all.

_____   You can conclude that

     A. Mary's talent suffered because of her blindness
     B. Mary joined the army in World War I
     C. most of Mary's paintings were of soldiers
     D. Mary's paintings were not very good

3. Most places on the seashore have two daily tides. They are known as high tide and low tide. Usually the difference between the water level of these two tides is only three or four feet. But a place in Canada has a great difference in tides. At the Bay of Fundy in Nova Scotia, the difference in tides is more than fifty feet.

_____   The story suggests that the Bay of Fundy

     A. is in South Carolina
     B. has ten tides daily
     C. is not near the seashore
     D. has unusual tides

Name _____   Date _____

Read the story. Choose the answer that best completes the sentence.

1. William Bligh was the cruel captain of a ship named the *Bounty*. He treated his sailors very badly. In 1789 the sailors couldn't take any more cruelty. By staging a mutiny and taking control of the ship, they put Bligh and 18 others into a small boat. But Bligh was able to sail the boat 4,000 miles across the Pacific to safety.

_____   The story suggests that Captain Bligh

    A. was a good sailor

    B. treated his crew well

    C. was popular with his crew

    D. did not lose control of his ship

2. There was a small Russian girl at the 1972 Olympics. She stood bravely before a huge audience and began her performance. She tumbled, leaped, flipped, and danced. She did somersaults and other difficult gymnastics exercises. In spite of her clean moves, the small girl did not win any medals at the end of the contest. But Olga Korbut had won the hearts of people all over the world.

_____   You can conclude that

    A. Korbut was a weightlifter

    B. the crowd cheered for Korbut

    C. Korbut won a gold medal

    D. the small girl fell down often

3. The Trail of Tears marked a sad event in Native American history. The Cherokee tribe lived in the southeast part of the country. But white settlers wanted them to move. The government ordered the Cherokee to leave their homes. They were told to move to Oklahoma. They didn't want to leave, but after some time they agreed. The trip was long and hard. Finally in March 1839, the tribe reached its new home. But more than three thousand Cherokee had died on the trip.

_____   You can tell from the story that

    A. the Cherokee liked their home in the southeast

    B. the tribe enjoyed the long journey

    C. the Cherokee never reached Oklahoma

    D. the white settlers liked the Cherokee

Name _____   Date _____

Read the story. Choose the answer that best completes the sentence.

1. The man carefully eyed the painting in the flea market. The picture was torn, but the frame was in good shape. The man decided to pay the asking price of four dollars. Later when the man removed the picture from the frame, he found an old piece of paper. The man's eyes widened in surprise because he had found an original copy of the Declaration of Independence. It was worth one million dollars!

_____   You can conclude that
    A. the man always had rotten luck
    B. the old piece of paper was a restaurant menu
    C. the man was glad that he bought the painting
    D. the frame was worth one million dollars

2. Charles Edensaw was a member of the Haida tribe. He lived in western Canada. Edensaw became a fine artist. He used wood, gold, and silver in his works. He was also a talented crafter of argillite, which is a kind of shale. His art included drawings, sketches, pipes, and totem poles. Today many of his works are found in museums.

_____   From this story you can tell that
    A. Charles Edensaw was a successful artist
    B. all of Edensaw's works are missing today
    C. Edensaw used only crayons in his works
    D. the Haida tribe lived in Kansas

3. Sonja Henie was one of the best ice-skaters of all time. Her first major contest was the 1924 Winter Olympics. Henie was just 12 years old! She won gold medals in the next 3 Olympics. She even won 10 world titles in a row. Then Henie became a movie star. Her movies often showed her skating. As a result, ice-skating was soon a popular sport around the world.

_____   From the story you <u>cannot</u> tell
    A. which sport Henie was best at
    B. how many movies Henie made
    C. when Henie's first major contest took place
    D. how many world titles Henie won in a row

         Comprehension 6, SV 6188-5

Name _____   Date _____

Read the story. Choose the answer that best completes the sentence.

1. Sandra Day O'Connor attended college and became a lawyer. But after she graduated, she couldn't find a job. Most law firms wouldn't hire female lawyers. O'Connor wanted to change this unfairness. First she was elected to the Arizona Senate. Then she became a judge. She was chosen to serve on the United States Supreme Court in 1981 and became the first woman to achieve this honor.

_____   From the story you <u>cannot</u> tell

    A. what Sandra O'Connor studied in college

    B. for which state she was senator

    C. when she joined the Supreme Court

    D. which college O'Connor attended

2. Have you ever had a nightmare? This kind of horrible dream can cause you to wake up screaming and breathing hard. The word *nightmare* comes from an ancient Saxon legend. The Saxons believed that Mara was an evil spirit that crouched on the chests of sleeping people and made their sleep very uncomfortable.

_____   You can tell from the story that

    A. nightmares were named after Mara

    B. Mara was a spirit in Spanish legends

    C. nightmares make people happy

    D. Mara sat on the pillows of sleeping people

3. Hazel Wightman was one of America's early tennis champions. She first played the game in 1902. Six months later she won her first tournament. Her last tournament win took place more than 50 years later. During her years of play, she came up with many new ways to play the game better. She used her skills to teach others how to play. Wightman was still teaching tennis when she died at age 87.

_____   The story suggests that

    A. Wightman is still alive

    B. tennis played a big part in Wightman's life

    C. Wightman was never very good at tennis

    D. Wightman played tennis only for a short while

Name _____   Date _____

Read the story. Choose the answer that best completes the sentence.

_____

1. The Ghost Dance is a traditional dance among many Native American tribes. Legend claims that the dance was begun by a Paiute named Wovoka, who had spoken to the Great Spirit. The Great Spirit advised the Paiute to be good and to live in peace. He presented Wovoka with the dance and told him that if the tribe danced for five nights, they would gain happiness. He also told him that the spirits of the dead would join the tribe.

_____   The story suggests that the Ghost Dance

    A. would bring good luck to a tribe

    B. was danced only by ghosts

    C. was given to Wovoka by the Great Turtle

    D. would cause people to die

_____

2. For many years bowling alleys were not considered proper places for women, but Floretta McCutcheon changed all that. She began bowling in 1923, and within four years she was the best bowler in her town. Then she challenged Jimmy Smith, the world champion. When the match was over, Floretta had won! Later she toured the nation, giving lessons and putting on bowling shows. She had many bowling fans.

_____   From the story you <u>cannot</u> tell

    A. when McCutcheon began to bowl

    B. which world champion McCutcheon defeated

    C. the town in which McCutcheon lived

    D. the kind of shows McCutcheon put on

_____

3. In the 1860s two crews set out to build a railroad. It would cross the western United States. One crew started laying tracks in Nebraska. The other crew began its work in California. Building the railroad took four years. The two crews met at Promontory Point, Utah, in May 1869. A golden spike was driven into the ground. The spike honored the completion of the railroad.

_____   From the story you can tell that

    A. the railroad crossed western Canada

    B. the two crews worked in directions toward each other

    C. the golden spike was driven in Nebraska

    D. Promontory Point is in California

_____

80   Comprehension 6, SV 6188-5

Name _____   Date _____

Read the story. Mark whether each statement is an inference or a fact.

---

1. During World War I, sheep roamed the White House lawn. The sheep were President Wilson's attempt to help the war effort. Since the sheep kept the grass short, the regular gardeners were not needed. They could be sent to the military. But not everyone liked the sheep. One reason was that the sheep ate the lawn's bushes and flowers. The president defended the use of the sheep. He said they also provided wool for blankets for the Red Cross.

Fact   Inference

○   ○   **A.** The sheep provided wool.

○   ○   **B.** President Wilson liked the sheep.

○   ○   **C.** The gardeners could be sent to the military.

○   ○   **D.** The sheep kept the grass short.

---

2. Ancient doctors believed that the human body was controlled by four liquids. They called these liquids blood, phlegm, black bile, and yellow bile. They were known as the four humors. The doctors believed that these four humors needed to be in balance. If they were not, then disease and pain filled the body.

Fact   Inference

○   ○   **A.** Doctors thought humors controlled the body.

○   ○   **B.** Blood was one of the four humors.

○   ○   **C.** Doctors tried to keep the humors balanced.

○   ○   **D.** Today doctors don't believe in humors.

---

3. In Greek legends Persephone was a pretty girl who loved the springtime and the outdoors. She was the daughter of Demeter, the goddess of the harvest. One day as the girl picked flowers on Earth, a great cart rumbled by her. In it was Hades, king of the underworld. He grabbed the girl and carried her to his world of dark caves deep below the earth. Persephone wanted to return to her mother. But Hades had fallen in love with the girl. So the young girl who loved sunshine was made the queen of the cold underworld.

Fact   Inference

○   ○   **A.** Persephone was made queen of the underworld.

○   ○   **B.** Hades forced Persephone to stay with him.

○   ○   **C.** Persephone did not like the underworld.

○   ○   **D.** Demeter was the mother of Persephone.

Go on to the next page.

Name _____   Date _____

4. Jules Verne is known as the father of science-fiction writing. Verne's books contained many ideas about future inventions and events. For example, in 1870 he wrote about moon travel in *From the Earth to the Moon*. His ideas were years ahead of their time. Verne died in 1905.

Fact Inference

○   ○   **A.** Verne was interested in the future.
○   ○   **B.** He is called the father of science fiction.
○   ○   **C.** The first flight to the moon was after 1870.
○   ○   **D.** Verne died in 1905.

5. Hibernating is similar to sleeping. Some animals undergo this process every winter. For several weeks before it hibernates, an animal eats more than it usually does. This allows its body to store fat. During hibernation the animal's body temperature drops. Lowering its body temperature helps an animal save its energy. Hibernating prevents the animal from starving when food is scarce.

Fact Inference

○   ○   **A.** Hibernating is similar to sleeping.
○   ○   **B.** Animals eat more before they hibernate.
○   ○   **C.** Some animals hibernate each winter.
○   ○   **D.** Before hibernation begins, food is easy to find.

6. The human heart beats sixty to seventy times a minute on average. Even when you are sleeping, your heart keeps up its important work. If you live to be seventy years old, your heart will do a lot of work. In seventy years a heart beats almost three billion times.

Fact Inference

○   ○   **A.** Your heart beats when you are asleep.
○   ○   **B.** The heart never rests.
○   ○   **C.** Healthy hearts must beat at a certain speed.
○   ○   **D.** The heart beats sixty to seventy times
             a minute.

Name _____   Date _____

Read the story. Mark whether each statement is an inference or a fact.

1. Edith Cavell was a famous British nurse. She was the head of a hospital in Belgium. When World War I broke out, Belgium was occupied by the Germans. Most of the wounded soldiers brought to the hospital were Allies. After they were well, Cavell helped them escape to safety in Holland. The hospital became an escape route from the Germans for hundreds of soldiers. But Cavell's secret was soon found out. In 1915 Cavell was shot by a German firing squad.

Fact Inference

○   ○   **A.** Cavell was a nurse in World War I.
○   ○   **B.** Belgium was occupied by the Germans.
○   ○   **C.** The Germans were angry with Cavell.
○   ○   **D.** Cavell agreed with the Allied cause.

2. Have you ever heard of the dog days of summer? They come between early July and late August. These days are often hot and sticky. Many people think they are called the dog days because they are not fit for a dog. In fact, though, the dog days have to do with the rising of the star Sirius. Sirius is also known as the Dog Star. The early Romans believed that this bright star added its heat to the sun to cause the high temperatures of the dog days.

Fact Inference

○   ○   **A.** Sirius first rises in early July.
○   ○   **B.** The dog days are in the summer.
○   ○   **C.** Sirius is known as the Dog Star.
○   ○   **D.** The dog days are often hot and sticky.

3. Sir Francis Drake was a famous English sailor. He first sailed the seas as a pirate, robbing Spanish ships. He gave the treasures he stole to Queen Elizabeth of England. She later made Drake a knight. Drake then set out on his ship, *The Golden Hind*, to sail around the world. He finished the voyage in 1580. Eight years later he helped to defend the English navy against the Spanish Armada.

Fact Inference

○   ○   **A.** Drake was an English sailor.
○   ○   **B.** *The Golden Hind* was Drake's ship.
○   ○   **C.** Queen Elizabeth appreciated Drake's efforts.
○   ○   **D.** Drake was a good sailor.

Name _____   Date _____

Read the story. Mark whether each statement is an inference or a fact.

1. Some animals make long journeys to escape cold or to find food. For example, a gray whale can travel up to 5,600 miles. Bats have been known to travel as far as 1,500 miles, and the record distance traveled by a butterfly is 4,000 miles. For toads the record is 2 miles. This may not seem like much, but that's a lot of hopping!

Fact Inference
○   ○   **A.** A butterfly has traveled 4,000 miles.
○   ○   **B.** Some animals travel to escape cold.
○   ○   **C.** Scientists can track how far an animal travels.
○   ○   **D.** Some bats have traveled 1,500 miles.

2. Have you ever heard of a "swan song"? This saying means a farewell appearance or a final act. The saying comes from an ancient legend about swans. It was once thought that a swan would remain silent all its life. But when it was dying, it would sing out in its final minutes. This swan song would be one of great feeling and beauty.

Fact Inference
○   ○   **A.** Ancient people thought swans were special.
○   ○   **B.** A "swan song" means a final act.
○   ○   **C.** Swans were supposedly silent until
             near death.
○   ○   **D.** The swan's final song was supposed to be very beautiful.

3. The date was January 10, 1901. Captain Anthony Lucas had his men hard at work in the Spindletop oil field in Texas. Suddenly their equipment began to shake. Then oil gushed from the ground, shooting high into the air. Everything nearby was coated with the thick, black oil. But Lucas and his men didn't mind. They had struck oil! Spindletop soon became one of the highest-producing oil fields in the world.

Fact Inference
○   ○   **A.** The Spindletop oil field was in Texas.
○   ○   **B.** Captain Lucas knew a lot about oil wells.
○   ○   **C.** Lucas and his men found oil.
○   ○   **D.** It was exciting when the men struck oil.

84

Name _____   Date _____

Read the story. Mark whether each statement is an inference or a fact.

---

1. Dave had just become a teenager. So he thought he was old enough to be treated as an adult, and he wanted to do things adults did. One day Dave decided he was going to drive his dad's car around the block. His parents were gone, and Dave knew he shouldn't touch the car. But he thought nobody would find out, so he got the keys and climbed into the car. He started the car, backed out of the driveway, and ran right into a fire hydrant on the other side of the street. Dave bumped his head on the steering wheel as water sprayed over the car.

Fact Inference

○   ○   **A.** Dave is a teenager.
○   ○   **B.** He wanted to be treated like an adult.
○   ○   **C.** Dave doesn't know how to drive.
○   ○   **D.** His parents were angry that he took the car.

---

2. How long can you swim before you get tired? Could you swim eight months without touching land? Alaskan seals can. In summer they live off the Alaskan coast, where their babies are born. Then the seals swim south before the cold Arctic winter sets in. They often swim over six thousand miles before returning to Alaska in the spring.

Fact Inference

○   ○   **A.** Alaskan seals can swim over 6,000 miles.
○   ○   **B.** Baby seals are born in Alaska.
○   ○   **C.** Alaskan seals don't like the Arctic winter.
○   ○   **D.** The seals return to Alaska in the spring.

---

3. Walt Whitman was a great American poet. As a young man, he was a teacher. Later he served as a nurse in the Civil War. Throughout his life he wrote poems. He often wrote in a new style called free verse. His poems sang the praises of America, freedom, and the common person. His most famous work is a book of poems called *Leaves of Grass*.

Fact Inference

○   ○   **A.** Whitman enjoyed writing poems.
○   ○   **B.** He served as a nurse in the Civil War.
○   ○   **C.** Whitman often wrote poems in free verse.
○   ○   **D.** He was proud of his country.

Name _____   Date _____

Read the story. Mark whether each statement is an inference or a fact.

1. The bell rang sharply in the middle of the night. Missy sat upright in her bed, rubbing her eyes. Again the sharp ringing split the silence. Trying to pull herself together, Missy scrambled for the phone. She had no idea who could be calling at that time of night, but she hoped it was not an emergency. When she answered the phone, a voice at the other end asked for someone named Felix. Disgusted, Missy said that Felix did not live there. Then the person on the other end slammed down the phone.

Fact Inference
○   ○   **A.** Missy was asleep when the phone rang.
○   ○   **B.** The other person dialed a wrong number.
○   ○   **C.** The phone rang in the middle of the night.
○   ○   **D.** The other person did not apologize.

2. In July 1969 a spaceship rushed toward the moon. The ship was called *Apollo 11*. On board were three men. They were Michael Collins, Neil Armstrong, and Edwin Aldrin, Jr. When the spaceship neared the moon, it began to orbit. Then a smaller craft carried two men to the moon's surface. Neil Armstrong became the first man to walk on the moon. He was soon followed by Edwin Aldrin, Jr.

Fact Inference
○   ○   **A.** *Apollo 11* went to the moon.
○   ○   **B.** Three men were on *Apollo 11*.
○   ○   **C.** Armstrong was the first to walk on the moon.
○   ○   **D.** Collins remained on the spaceship.

3. *Dandelion* was first a French word. It refers to a part of a lion. Long ago the flower was called "lion's tooth" because of the leaf's shape. In French it was known as *dent de lion*, or tooth of the lion. After a while this became the English word *dandelion*.

Fact Inference
○   ○   **A.** *Dandelion* comes from a French word.
○   ○   **B.** In French the name meant "lion's tooth."
○   ○   **C.** Dandelions grow in France.
○   ○   **D.** People thought the leaf looked like a tooth.

Name _____   Date _____

Read the story. Mark whether each statement is an inference or a fact.

1. Jomo Kenyatta hoped the people of Africa would one day be free. He worked very hard to gain rights for his tribe in Kenya. Then he was put in jail by the British and charged with causing trouble in Kenya. During his years in jail, his country moved toward freedom. Kenyatta was freed in 1961. He soon was named president of the new free nation of Kenya.

Fact   Inference
○   ○   **A.** Kenyatta was released from jail in 1961.
○   ○   **B.** The British once ruled Kenya.
○   ○   **C.** Kenyatta was charged with causing trouble.
○   ○   **D.** He became president of Kenya.

2. Have you ever heard of a "baker's dozen"? This saying means 13 of something. The saying is about 500 years old. Bakers then did not weigh their bread correctly. They tried to cheat their customers. So laws were passed to make the bakers give their customers the correct amount of bread for their money. The bakers could not bake a loaf of bread to weigh an exact amount. So bakers started giving 13 loaves of bread for each order of 12. This would make sure the bread weighed enough.

Fact   Inference
○   ○   **A.** Bakers once sold bread by weight.
○   ○   **B.** A baker's dozen is 13 of something.
○   ○   **C.** The saying is 500 years old.
○   ○   **D.** The bakers wanted to obey the new law.

3. Ada Lovelace was the daughter of the great poet Lord Byron. But she was famous in her own right. She became an expert in math at a very young age. Lovelace taught herself most of what she knew of the subject. She figured out how a computer would work a century before its invention. She also saw that such a machine could only "do whatever we know how to order it to perform." This is the key to modern computer programming.

Fact   Inference
○   ○   **A.** Ada Lovelace was the child of Lord Byron.
○   ○   **B.** Lord Byron was a great poet.
○   ○   **C.** Ada Lovelace did not want to be a poet.
○   ○   **D.** Ada Lovelace was a very smart person.

         Comprehension 6, SV 6188-5

Name _____   Date _____

Read the story. Mark whether each statement is an inference or a fact.

---

1. The ostrich is the largest bird in the world. It can grow to more than nine feet tall. Although ostriches cannot fly, these African birds can run quite fast. Their highest speed is about 40 miles per hour. Ostrich eggs are very large and weigh about 4 pounds. That's 24 times as heavy as a chicken egg!

Fact   Inference

○   ○   A. Chicken eggs are much smaller than ostrich eggs.

○   ○   B. Ostriches cannot fly.

○   ○   C. Nine feet high is very tall for a bird.

○   ○   D. Ostriches can run up to 40 miles an hour.

---

2. The nursery rhyme "Humpty Dumpty" may have been written about King Richard III of England. The king was hump-backed and had a horse named Wall. When King Richard lost an important battle, he lost his position as king. It is perhaps this event that the rhyme talks about in the line "Humpty Dumpty had a great fall."

Fact   Inference

○   ○   A. "Humpty Dumpty" is a rhyme.

○   ○   B. It was important for kings to win in battle.

○   ○   C. King Richard III had a horse named Wall.

○   ○   D. Richard III was once the king of England.

---

3. Burt had played the saxophone for three years. This year he got up the courage to try out for the jazz band. For weeks before the tryout, he practiced every day after school for an hour. On the day of the tryout, he was very nervous and did not do well. When he found out he did not make the jazz band, he was very disappointed. A few weeks later, the music teacher decided another sax was needed, and she asked Burt to join the jazz band.

Fact   Inference

○   ○   A. Burt really wanted to be in the jazz band.

○   ○   B. Burt plays the saxophone.

○   ○   C. Burt was disappointed about not being chosen.

○   ○   D. The teacher asked Burt to join the band.

Name _____   Date _____

Read the story. Mark whether each statement is an inference or a fact.

1. Ruth's hobby was making radio-controlled airplanes. But even more than making them, she enjoyed flying the planes. Once Ruth spent every weekend for an entire month working with her dad to build an airplane. The next Saturday Ruth decided to try out the plane. When Ruth set up the airplane for takeoff, she didn't notice the tall pine trees standing in its path.

Fact   Inference

○   ○   **A.** Ruth enjoys flying radio-controlled planes.

○   ○   **B.** Tall trees were in the path of the plane.

○   ○   **C.** The airplane crashed in the trees.

○   ○   **D.** Ruth worked with her dad to build a plane.

2. Crocodiles lay their eggs in sand. Three months later the eggs are ready to hatch. The baby crocodiles are too weak to dig out the sand around them, so they start to peep from inside their shells. Their mother, who has never strayed very far away, hears the calls and digs the eggs out.

Fact   Inference

○   ○   **A.** The mother stays nearby so she can hear the babies.

○   ○   **B.** The babies have loud voices.

○   ○   **C.** Sand protects the crocodile eggs.

○   ○   **D.** The mother digs the eggs out.

3. Have you ever thought about how keys open doors? A key is cut a special way so that it matches the pattern of its lock. Inside the lock there is a metal bar. A row of pins holds the bar in place. When the matching key is put into the lock, it raises the pins and allows the bar to move. The bar then slides out of the way and unlocks the door when the key is turned.

Fact   Inference

○   ○   **A.** Keys are cut a special way.

○   ○   **B.** A metal bar is inside the lock.

○   ○   **C.** The bar keeps the door locked.

○   ○   **D.** The wrong key won't raise a lock's pins.

Name _____   Date _____

Read the story. Mark whether each statement is an inference or a fact.

1. James and Jenny wanted to give their mom a special birthday present. "I have an idea," James said. "We could clean the whole house from top to bottom." "You're right! Mom would never believe it!" Jenny said. The next Saturday they asked their dad to take their mom out all afternoon. They vacuumed, dusted, and washed floors and windows until the whole house sparkled.

Fact   Inference
○   ○   A. James and Jenny cleaned the house.
○   ○   B. Their mom was surprised.
○   ○   C. James and Jenny love their mom.
○   ○   D. They were tired after working all afternoon.

2. Daniel Defoe wrote the book *Robinson Crusoe*. He got his ideas from the real-life adventures of a man named Alexander Selkirk. Selkirk was a sailor on a ship off the coast of Chile. In 1704 he argued with his captain and demanded to be left on shore. The captain allowed Selkirk to stay. Selkirk lived by eating turtles, fish, and goats. He was finally rescued in 1709.

Fact   Inference
○   ○   A. Selkirk was a stubborn man.
○   ○   B. The captain allowed Selkirk to stay.
○   ○   C. Daniel Defoe wrote *Robinson Crusoe*.
○   ○   D. Selkirk became good at hunting and fishing.

3. Michael loved the cool, crisp, fall weather so much that he actually enjoyed raking leaves. One day he noticed that Mr. Longly's yard down the road was full of leaves. Michael knew that Mr. Longly used a wheelchair to get around. That day after school, Michael picked up his rake and headed for Mr. Longly's house.

Fact   Inference
○   ○   A. Michael loved fall weather.
○   ○   B. Mr. Longly used a wheelchair.
○   ○   C. Michael raked Mr. Longly's leaves for him.
○   ○   D. Mr. Longly's yard was down the road.

Name _____   Date _____

Read the story. Mark whether each statement is an inference or a fact.

1. When she was a girl, Marian Anderson dreamed of becoming a famous concert singer. But in those days, that dream seemed impossible for someone who was both poor and black. When she was seventeen, she began studying with a famous voice teacher. Within a year she performed throughout the South in her first concert tour. In the 1930s she sang all over the world. In 1963 President Lyndon Johnson awarded her the Presidential Medal of Freedom.

Fact   Inference
○   ○   **A.** Anderson was a talented singer.
○   ○   **B.** A famous teacher gave Anderson lessons.
○   ○   **C.** Anderson was respected by many people.
○   ○   **D.** President Johnson gave Anderson an award.

2. Camels do not need much water. During the cool months in the desert, they usually do not drink water since they get enough from the plants they eat. When the temperature is around 95 degrees, they can go about 15 days without a drink. When the temperature is 104 degrees, camels drink water whenever they can.

Fact   Inference
○   ○   **A.** Camels need more water in hotter weather.
○   ○   **B.** Camels can go 15 days without a drink.
○   ○   **C.** Eating plants provides camels with water.
○   ○   **D.** Camels are used to living in dry climates.

3. Patty and her mom were very excited to plant their first garden. They looked forward to growing their own vegetables. First they used a hoe to prepare the soil. Then they added peat moss to the soil. They planted tomatoes, lettuce, beans, and peas. Every week Patty spent at least an hour weeding and watering the plants. At the end of the summer, Patty shared the vegetables with her friends.

Fact   Inference
○   ○   **A.** Patty planted tomatoes in her garden.
○   ○   **B.** They prepared the soil with a hoe.
○   ○   **C.** Her friends appreciated the vegetables.
○   ○   **D.** Patty is a hard worker.

Name _____   Date _____

Read the story. Mark whether each statement is an inference or a fact.

1. Late one evening Seth was waiting for a bus downtown. While he waited he heard a swooshing sound behind him. As he turned around, he saw two teenage boys spray-painting words on a fence. When the boys saw him, they ran away. Seth was able to remember what they looked like. He helped the police determine who the two boys were.

Fact   Inference
○   ○   A. Seth has a good memory.
○   ○   B. He was waiting for a bus.
○   ○   C. The boys were afraid when Seth saw them.
○   ○   D. Seth heard a swooshing sound.

2. Kites were probably first made in China over 2,500 years ago. The first kites were large leaves with lines of twisted vines. Today the most common types of kites are the flat kite, the box kite, and the bowed kite. Some kites look like ships or airplanes or even animals. A dragon kite is a very popular type of animal kite.

Fact   Inference
○   ○   A. The box kite is a common type of kite.
○   ○   B. Many people like the way dragon kites look.
○   ○   C. Today kites aren't made of leaves and vines.
○   ○   D. Kites were probably first made in China.

3. Most people think of Betsy Ross as the designer of the American flag. But Betsy Ross probably just sewed a design that Francis Hopkinson developed in 1776. Thirty years afterward Ross's grandson claimed that his grandmother was visited by a secret group that included George Washington. Supposedly at that meeting, Washington asked her to design and sew America's first flag.

Fact   Inference
○   ○   A. Hopkinson developed a design in 1776.
○   ○   B. Ross's grandson said she designed the American flag.
○   ○   C. Most people think Ross designed the American flag.
○   ○   D. It's not clear who designed the American flag.

         Comprehension 6, SV 6188-5

Name _____   Date _____

Read the story. Mark whether each statement is an inference or a fact.

1. Michelle had stayed at Marla's house much longer than she had planned. Now it was beginning to get dark outside. She said goodbye and got on her bike to go home. As she was riding, it grew darker and darker. She could barely see five feet in front of her, so she rode very slowly. When she finally got to her street, she felt a great sense of relief.

Fact   Inference
○   ○   **A.** It was beginning to get dark.
○   ○   **B.** Michelle rode her bike home.
○   ○   **C.** She felt a little scared.
○   ○   **D.** Michelle wished she had left earlier.

2. Chip's family was at the beach. His grandmother had planned to go but couldn't at the last minute because of health problems. Chip remembered how she would let him look at her shell collection when he was younger. He used to enjoy holding the big conch shell up to his ears to hear the sea. The day before his family planned to return home, Chip went out early in the morning and picked up several interesting shells for his grandmother.

Fact   Inference
○   ○   **A.** Chip was at the beach.
○   ○   **B.** Chip's grandmother couldn't go with the family.
○   ○   **C.** Chip's grandmother liked shells.
○   ○   **D.** Chip missed his grandmother.

3. The United States government records thousands of inventions each year. One of the strangest was eyeglasses for chickens. Because chickens peck each other, one inventor had the idea of making special protective glasses for chickens. They were designed to fit around the back of the chicken's neck.

Fact   Inference
○   ○   **A.** Chickens pecking each other is a problem.
○   ○   **B.** The glasses fit around the chicken's neck.
○   ○   **C.** The government records inventions.
○   ○   **D.** The glasses did not become popular.

Name _____   Date _____

Read the story. Mark whether each statement is an inference or a fact.

1.   Wilt Chamberlain holds the record for scoring the most points in one professional basketball game. In 1962 the Philadelphia Warrior scored 100 points against the New York Knicks. Chamberlain's record was 29 points higher than the record of the next-highest scorer.

Fact   Inference
○   ○   A. Chamberlain played professional basketball.
○   ○   B. Chamberlain scored 100 points in one game.
○   ○   C. Chamberlain was a very good player.
○   ○   D. Chamberlain's record will be hard to beat.

2.   All of Lou's friends had been invited to Molly's birthday party. Lou expected to be invited, too. But after several days of not getting an invitation, Lou guessed that she was not invited. The day after the party, Molly asked Lou why she didn't come. Lou told Molly that she had not been invited. Molly explained that she had put the invitation in Lou's desk at school. Lou then looked through her desk and found a sealed envelope with her name on it.

Fact   Inference
○   ○   A. Molly was surprised when Lou did not come.
○   ○   B. Lou found the envelope in her desk.
○   ○   C. Molly told Lou where the invitation was.
○   ○   D. Lou wanted to be invited to the party.

3.   Lightning seems to flash a few seconds before you hear the thunder it makes. The reason for this is that light travels much faster than sound. Actually the thunder happens at the same instant as the lightning. Thunder is caused when the lightning heats up the air so fast that there is an explosion.

Fact   Inference
○   ○   A. Air is heated by lightning.
○   ○   B. Thunder happens at the same time as lightning.
○   ○   C. Light travels faster than sound.
○   ○   D. Thunder is caused by an explosion.

94   Comprehension 6, SV 6188-5

COMPREHENSION: GRADE 6
ANSWER KEY

Unit I: Facts
Assessment, pp. 11-12
1. C
2. B
3. A
4. C
5. B
6. D
7. B
8. A
9. C
10. B

Lesson 1, pp. 13-14
1. C
2. A
3. D
4. B
5. D
6. C
7. D
8. A
9. B
10. A

Lesson 2, pp. 15-16
1. D
2. B
3. A
4. B
5. A
6. B
7. A
8. C
9. D
10. C

Lesson 3, pp. 17-18
1. C
2. A
3. B
4. D
5. C
6. A
7. C
8. B
9. D
10. D

Lesson 4, pp. 19-20
1. A
2. C
3. B
4. D
5. C
6. B
7. B
8. D
9. D
10. A

Lesson 5, pp. 21-22
1. C
2. A
3. C
4. D
5. B
6. D
7. C
8. D
9. A
10. B

Lesson 6, pp. 23-24
1. C
2. D
3. D
4. B
5. A
6. A
7. A
8. B
9. D
10. C

Unit II: Sequence
Assessment, p. 26
1. 3, 1, 2
2. B
3. A
4. C
5. C

Lesson 1, p. 28
1. 3, 1, 2
2. C
3. B
4. A
5. A

Lesson 2, p. 30
1. 3, 2, 1
2. B
3. A
4. C
5. A

Lesson 3, p. 32
1. 3, 1, 2
2. B
3. C
4. C
5. B

Lesson 4, p. 34
1. 2, 1, 3
2. B
3. C
4. A
5. B

Lesson 5, p. 36
1. 1, 3, 2
2. A
3. A
4. B
5. C

Lesson 6, p. 38
1. 3, 2, 1
2. C
3. A
4. B
5. C

Unit III: Context
Assessment, pp. 39-40
1. B
2. C
3. D
4. A
5. B
6. D
7. C
8. D
9. C
10. D

11. C
12. D

Lesson 1, p. 41
1. A
2. C
3. A
4. C
5. D
6. B
7. B
8. C

Lesson 2, p. 42
1. C
2. C
3. B
4. D
5. A
6. A
7. D
8. B

Lesson 3, p. 43
1. B
2. D
3. D
4. A
5. D
6. C
7. D
8. A

Lesson 4, p. 44
1. C
2. B
3. C
4. A
5. A
6. C
7. C
8. B

Lesson 5, p. 45
1. D
2. C
3. C
4. D
5. B
6. A
7. A
8. C

Lesson 6, p. 46
1. B
2. A
3. D
4. C
5. B
6. C
7. A
8. C

Lesson 7, p. 47
1. B
2. D
3. C
4. C

Lesson 8, p. 48
1. D
2. D
3. A
4. B

Lesson 9, p. 49
1. C
2. C
3. B
4. A

Lesson 10, p. 50
1. C
2. A
3. C
4. D

Lesson 11, p. 51
1. D
2. A
3. B
4. D

Lesson 12, p. 52
1. D
2. C
3. B
4. A

Unit IV: Main Idea
Assessment, pp. 53-54
1. C
2. B
3. C
4. C
5. C
6. B

Lesson 1, p. 55
1. B
2. A
3. C

Lesson 2, p. 56
1. A
2. D
3. D

Lesson 3, p. 57
1. C
2. D
3. B

Lesson 4, p. 58
1. A
2. B
3. C

Lesson 5, p. 59
1. C
2. C
3. A

Lesson 6, p. 60
1. A
2. B
3. B

Lesson 7, p. 61
1. B
2. A
3. D

Lesson 8, p. 62
1. A
2. A
3. B

Comprehension 6, SV 6188-5

Lesson 9, p. 63
1. C
2. A
3. A

Lesson 10, p. 64
1. B
2. A
3. C

Lesson 11, p. 65
1. D
2. A
3. C

Lesson 12, p. 66
1. D
2. C
3. B

Unit V: Conclusion
Assessment, pp. 67-68
1. C
2. A
3. D
4. C
5. B
6. A

Lesson 1, p. 69
1. C
2. C
3. B

Lesson 2, p. 70
1. A
2. C
3. B

Lesson 3, p. 71
1. C
2. B
3. D

Lesson 4, p. 72
1. B
2. A
3. C

Lesson 5, p. 73
1. C
2. C
3. B

Lesson 6, p. 74
1. C
2. A
3. C

Lesson 7, p. 75
1. A
2. C
3. D

Lesson 8, p. 76
1. B
2. A
3. D

Lesson 9, p. 77
1. A
2. B
3. A

Lesson 10, p. 78
1. C
2. A
3. B

Lesson 11, p. 79
1. D
2. A
3. B

Lesson 12, p. 80
1. A
2. C
3. B

Unit VI: Inference
Assessment, pp. 81-82
1. A. F
   B. I
   C. F
   D. F
2. A. F
   B. F
   C. I
   D. I
3. A. F
   B. I
   C. I
   D. F
4. A. I
   B. F
   C. I
   D. F
5. A. F
   B. F
   C. F
   D. I
6. A. F
   B. I
   C. I
   D. F

Lesson 1, p. 83
1. A. I
   B. F
   C. I
   D. I
2. A. I
   B. F
   C. F
   D. F
3. A. F
   B. F
   C. I
   D. I

Lesson 2, p. 84
1. A. F
   B. F
   C. I
   D. F
2. A. I
   B. F
   C. F
   D. F
3. A. F
   B. I
   C. F
   D. I

Lesson 3, p. 85
1. A. F
   B. I
   C. I
   D. I
2. A. F
   B. F
   C. I

D. F
3. A. I
   B. F
   C. F
   D. I

Lesson 4, p. 86
1. A. I
   B. I
   C. F
   D. I
2. A. F
   B. F
   C. F
   D. I
3. A. F
   B. F
   C. I
   D. I

Lesson 5, p. 87
1. A. F
   B. I
   C. F
   D. F
2. A. I
   B. F
   C. F
   D. I
3. A. F
   B. F
   C. I
   D. I

Lesson 6, p. 88
1. A. I
   B. F
   C. I
   D. F
2. A. F
   B. I
   C. F
   D. F
3. A. I
   B. F
   C. F
   D. F

Lesson 7, p. 89
1. A. F
   B. F
   C. I
   D. F
2. A. I
   B. I
   C. I
   D. F
3. A. F
   B. F
   C. I
   D. I

Lesson 8, p. 90
1. A. F
   B. I
   C. I
   D. I
2. A. I
   B. F
   C. F
   D. I
3. A. F
   B. F

C. I
D. F

Lesson 9, p. 91
1. A. I
   B. F
   C. I
   D. F
2. A. I
   B. F
   C. F
   D. I
3. A. F
   B. F
   C. I
   D. I

Lesson 10, p. 92
1. A. I
   B. F
   C. I
   D. F
2. A. F
   B. I
   C. I
   D. F
3. A. F
   B. F
   C. F
   D. I

Lesson 11, p. 93
1. A. F
   B. F
   C. I
   D. I
2. A. F
   B. F
   C. I
   D. I
3. A. I
   B. F
   C. F
   D. I

Lesson 12, p. 94
1. A. I
   B. F
   C. I
   D. I
2. A. I
   B. F
   C. F
   D. I
3. A. F
   B. F
   C. F
   D. F

© Steck-Vaughn Company   Comprehension 6, SV 6188-5